NEW ORDER

BALLANTINE BOOKS | NEW YORK

NEW ORDER

A DECLUTTERING HANDBOOK FOR CREATIVE FOLKS

(AND EVERYONE ELSE)

FAY WOLF

ILLUSTRATED BY JEREMY GATES

A Ballantine Books Trade Paperback Original

Published in the United States by Ballantine Books, an imprint of Random House, a division of Penguin Random House LLC, New York.

BALLANTINE and the HOUSE colophon are registered trademarks of Penguin Random House LLC.

ISBN 978-1-101-88619-9
ebook ISBN 978-1-101-88620-5

Illustrations by Jeremy Gates
jeremyjohngates.com

Printed in the United States of America on acid-free paper

randomhousebooks.com

2 4 6 8 9 7 5 3 1

For my father, Herman.
In honor of your expansive mind,
your kind and ageless heart,
your inspired collaborations with Bucky Fuller,
and your very messy desk.

Man is able to do more with less and less and less.

—R. BUCKMINSTER FULLER

WELCOME

Thanks for opening this handbook. And a high five for doing so. Perhaps you're here because you have an inkling that life might be a little sweeter if you had less stuff and more order. And you'd be right. **The decluttered life does indeed taste (a whole lot) better.**

I didn't know how *much* better until I started to teach it to others. For the past ten years, I've had the pleasure of helping hundreds of good people streamline their lives. From the outer clutter of closets and kitchens to the inner clutter of artists who are afraid to step out into their spotlights.

How'd I get into this biz? At the end of 2005, sparked by the loss of my supercool dad, I decided to get into the driver's seat of life. For me, that meant becoming my own boss. A small foray into personal assisting for some friends revealed that I had a knack for making sense of their papers and their lives. And when I learned that there was an occupation called "professional organizer," sweet choruses of angels began to sing. So I became one.

People regularly ask me, **"What's the craziest thing you've seen in some-**

one else's space?" And sure, I've seen a lot of intimate (and highly confidential) stuff—but it's usually the same as the next guy's. So that question kinda misses the point. The most *compelling* thing that I see, day in and day out, is that *almost every one of us* struggles with clutter and productivity, in a normal, everyday kind of way. We just don't talk about it. **It's not about other people. It's about *us*.** And our own deeply rooted emotions and fears surrounding what's ours.

   It's always hard to start. It feels overwhelming. It feels too precise and precious. It feels like a huge undertaking that you simply don't have time for. And it feels like if you haven't quite reached a *Hoarders*-level situation, then maybe you can put it off for another day or three. Kicking these kinds of thought patterns to the curb—and slamming the door behind them—is what lights me up. And that's just the beginning.

WHY CREATIVE FOLKS (AND EVERYONE ELSE)?

New Order has a bent toward the creative, whether that means clearing physical space to set up a drum kit in your living room, reclaiming mental space to let the great ideas flow, or paring down your schedule so you have time to go rock climbing once a month. This book is for anyone who wants to do, well, anything new or a little different from what you're doing now. The endgame is not just the cleared space and the slimmed-down inbox. **The endgame is how this new way of living makes you *feel*, how it allows you to *operate*, and what it *inspires you to do next*.**

DECLUTTERING IS A GATEWAY DRUG
(THE GOOD KIND)

I'm in deep love with my clients. I work with all genders, young and old, wealthy and scraping by. **Many are creative folks who know what it's like to encounter blocks to getting what they really want. And I'm one too.** While running New Order, my organizing business, I simultaneously enjoy a life as an artist, both as an actress and most recently as a singer-songwriter (to which you'll find a few allusions in the pages ahead). In other words, I'm right there in the trenches with you, figuring out in real time how to make the decluttered and multidisciplinary life a reality. It's an ongoing journey of discovery, and I'm thrilled to share some of the things that have worked for me, and for my clients, thus far.

Along the way, I've seen some pretty gratifying stuff: a corner heaped with piles of dirty laundry turned into a music nook, a dusty garage turned into a craft room, an overstuffed closet turned into a voiceover booth. The even *better* payoff is then seeing my clients' creative work flourish and grow as a direct result. And of course, I've witnessed a thousand smaller miracles, too, like the work-from-home parent whose day-to-day life greatly improved just by hanging up a simple corkboard (and using it).

By doing even *some* of this work, your life will actually change. For the better. Every time. So . . . there are only two ways this can go:

STAY THE SAME OR MAKE IT BETTER.

WELCOME TO YOUR NEW ORDER.

MY NAME IS FAY,
AND I'LL BE YOUR GUIDE.

CONTENTS

BEFORE YOU BEGIN

> YOUR FIRST STEP IS **NOT**
> TO GO TO THE STORE TO
> BUY ORGANIZING PRODUCTS.

RESIST, FRIEND.

I want *New Order* to move as quickly as possible for you. These are the wham-bam, fast-track basics to stepping up your decluttering game and getting all kindsa shit done.

So, enough small talk. Let's start with a few important tips, prompts, and principles to carry you through this book, and on to your less cluttered, more joyous life.

WHAT ARE YOU LOOKING FOR?

Maybe it's your keys or that piece of paper you wrote that important thing on. You could've sworn you just bought new shaving cream, but the drugstore bag has straight-up disappeared. Before we attack the specifics, let's take a few steps back to ask:

What are you *truly* looking for?

Perhaps something more along the lines of . . . Sharper clarity. Less anxiety. More control of your domain. More time (not spent looking for things). More money (not wasted on replacing stuff you can't find or are never going to use). A better handle on your many, many responsibilities. A road map for completing your beloved projects. Peace and quiet.

Great news! Those nebulous golden nuggets you're seeking? They *can* actually appear in the form of knowing where your keys are, which is inextricably linked to the peace, and to the quiet. The work we're about to do isn't just about seemingly boring tasks like sorting your bathroom cabinet. **As you take this journey, keep your eyes on the bigger prizes. You will be rewarded.**

SMALL STEPS

As you learn my trusted techniques, remember this all-important mantra: **Breaking down tasks and projects into bite-size pieces is the easiest, most efficient, least stressful way to complete them.** It's impossible to declutter your whole house *and* dive into all your old paperwork *and* reply to a backlog of 5,000 emails all in one day. So maybe today just start with one corner of the living room.

A little better is a little better.

You can start the book with any chapter or you can read it cover to cover. Chapters 1 and 2 go hand in hand. But otherwise: **take what you need and move along, friend.** No mastery required.

I'll also be sharing some of my favorite, tried-and-true apps, websites, and resources with you as we go, and you can find more information on all of them on page 173.

HOW LONG DO I DO IT FOR?

You can usually get more done than you think by committing to just 10, 20, or 30 minutes of dedicated purging. For instance: you are allowed—right this second—to walk over to your bookshelf, go down the rows left to right, and start saying goodbye. (Nope, you don't still need that novel from the book club you never attended. And you are still a smart person, even without a copy of *The Catcher in the Rye*.) If you're brutal, you'll be surprised by just how many go into the Donate pile, all in less than half an hour. It's cool; I'll wait.

If you're looking to really make some lasting magic happen in your clothes closet, office, art studio, etc., it'll be fruitful to set aside at least two hours. Depending on how much stuff you have, you may not "finish" in one afternoon, but you *will* make a noticeable dent. And that dent will inspire you to do more when you're able.

When it comes to physical space and paper (chapters 1, 2, and 3), always allow for clean-up time. Your closet/office/studio will most likely look worse before it gets better, but do not despair. If you are able to dig in for a few hours, allot about 30 minutes to put everything away. ("Away" can mean either *in its new home* or *neatly off to the side* if it's a project you'll be returning to.) You'll also use that time to bag up donations and get rid of trash and recycling.

All this said, the most important thing is to JUST START. What plagues so many of us is the "waiting for the perfect moment" and thus the "not doing anything about it." So ditch the excuses and start with *any* amount of time.

SET TIMERS

Timers are your new best friends. In fact, I've got my best friend counting down right now as I write this chapter. He keeps me on task and cuts down on distractions. And he's the only nonliving thing I've ever felt accountable to. The *ding* when the time's up gives me a huge sense of accomplishment and proves that I *can* make a lot of progress in a short amount of time. It's like your New Order boxing ring. *Ding:* **Time to fight.** *Ding:* **Time to quit.**

Pressing Start on a timer also keeps us healthier by forcing breaks. There's no need to power through. It's a marathon, not a sprint. You're allowed to take your time and refuel, and you'll actually be able to go for *longer* if you listen to your body's needs and attend to them. Timers remind you to do that.

SCREW PERFECTION

Perfect is the archenemy of Better. Perfect is boring. Perfect is unattainable. (Glossy magazines and slick TV shows rarely reflect real life.)

Your home and mind can be imperfectly beautiful . . . imperfectly *better*. **New Order will illustrate how. Let's jump in.**

NEW ORDER

LESS STUFF

SORT IT OUT + LET IT GO

Welcome to the road to Better. In this chapter alone, you'll learn how to completely declutter any spot you choose, so that all you're left with are the things you truly need and truly love. If you're looking for more *actual space* in your life so that you can spread out and write your masterpiece or effortlessly cook a decadent meal, start here.

SET UP & SORT

Choose ONE area to tackle: one closet, one surface, or one corner of your living room. Small steps to victory. It may be easier to start with the less emotional stuff (e.g., the kitchen table rather than the memorabilia passed down by your late grandpa), but there's no "right place" to begin. Just *start*.

Decide on a clear staging area. This is where you'll be sorting out all the things you decide to keep. A table, bed, or couch will do. A designated area of the floor will also work just fine. Can't find a staging area because there's too much stuff everywhere? It's okay to shove piles together for the purpose of clearing a space. Ideally, you're then going to sort through that very stuff anyway. **Set up the sorting bins nearby.** They're for quickly grouping all the clutter that's leaving your life for good. Yeah, you heard me.

WHAT YOU NEED

- A clear staging area
- Post-its
- A Sharpie
- Sorting bins

ALSO HELPFUL

- Rubber bands
- Scissors
- Stapler
- Tape
- Trash bags

Don't let a lack of having every single item on this list keep you from **STARTING**.

IMPROVISATION

IS ENCOURAGED.

SET UP YOUR SORTING BINS

There are five major categories I use when sorting:

- **Donate**

- **Trash**

- **Recycle**

- **Shred**

- **Other Rooms**

Each category has a bin.
Bin options:

1. **Cardboard boxes (or "Bankers Boxes").** Not only can these be used for sorting, but afterward they can turn into storage for items that need a new home.
2. **Laundry baskets or large containers** you already have around the house—provided it's not too time-consuming to free them up.
3. **Brown paper grocery bags.** Not the ideal level of sturdiness. But they'll work!
4. **No bins at all** (except for actual trash and recycling). Labeled—and clearly defined—piles are fine.

You can mix and match. Doesn't matter, as long as you use clear labels.

If you *really want* to purchase fancy sorting bins, grab some 16-inch Folding Mesh Cubes (see page 174 in Resources). They're inexpensive, sturdy, and reusable, and they take up almost no room to store. I recommend these as a long-term product to have on hand for ongoing decluttering and easy transport of donations and discards.

When you start purging, each discard will go into the **Donate, Trash, Recycle,** or **Shred** bin. (Shred will be a fuller bin when you're working exclusively with paper. But you never know what kind of sensitive info you might find among your clutter.)

Other Rooms

This bin is for items that actually *do* have a home, or some semblance of one, around the house. For instance, you've discovered your vintage Pyrex dish while decluttering the hall closet. Instead of messing with your momentum (and questioning how the heck it got there), chuck it into the Other Rooms bin and keep rolling.

LABEL YOUR SORTING BINS

Use Post-its to create labels for your sorting categories. Depending on the type of container you've got, you can either stick them right on or use a binder clip or clothespin to affix. Or feel free to cut out the labels on page 179 and match them up with the bins of your choosing.

START SORTING (AND SIMULTANEOUSLY PURGING)!

Put on some tunes, if you like. (Nothing *too* distracting, though.[1]) Commit to uninterrupted time. Set a timer. Aaaand . . . GO.

---

[1] Songza.com is always great for choosing a mood.

THE THREE STEPS OF SORTING

1. PICK UP ONE ITEM.
2. MAKE A DECISION.
3. PUT IT IN A BIN OR A PILE.

—— THE END ——

Move around your space (or desk or closet) from left to right. Or right to left. The point is to curb meandering. **Pick up one thing and make a decision. Then pick up the thing *that's right next to it*. And make a decision.**

If you're dealing with a hard-to-reach space, collect a handful at a time and bring it to the staging area. Taking everything out at once tends to create more "holy shit" overwhelm. Small. Steps.

The Purge is an all-important part of the sorting process. Most of what you're going through is stuff you're deciding to banish from your life forever and ever (*cackle, cackle*). Ideally, you're purging A LOT.

THE RULE FOR PURGING IS INCREDIBLY SIMPLE:

If you don't use and/or love it (and I mean **SUPERDUPERLOVE** it and would fall into a deep depression if it was gone), then you must let go of it and move forward with a less cluttered, more blissful life. Cool?

Questions to Keep in Mind

- Would you miss it if it was gone?
- Are you keeping it out of guilt?
- Are you indifferent to it?
- Would it make someone else happier than it makes you?
- Is it ripped or broken? (And: Are you really gonna fix it?)
- Would you rather have a better version of it?
- Do you have multiples of the same item?
- What are the chances you'll need one or four Ethernet cables ever again?
- Is it *expired*?
- Have you used it in the past year? Do you want to use it again?
- Have you worn it in the past year? Does it fit? (Do clothes that don't fit just make you feel bad about yourself?)
- Are you keeping it "just in case"? (Unless we're talking emergency supplies, please don't keep it.)
- Does it remind you of a shitty memory?
- Or, if it's a happy memory, how many other possessions remind you of that same experience?
- Does this thing represent your true self / tell the truth of who you are? No? Get rid of it.

P.S. What do you need all this stuff for?

Be brutal with yourself. Your (more joyous) life literally depends on it.

PRO TIP

Purging clothes? Empty the pockets. Sometimes you'll find beloved stuff in there. Or money!

THE KEEPERS

For some folks, the letting-go is easy. But what about the stuff you're keeping? On your staging area, sort the Keepers into smaller categories. Remember: these are items you use and/or superlove. Put like items together: batteries with batteries; extra staples with pencils, perhaps, in an Office Supplies category; Band-Aids and Neosporin both in First Aid.

Using Post-its to quickly label new categories as they come up will bring peace of mind throughout the process. For instance, decluttering a packed clothes closet may take two days to complete, and you need to sleep on the very bed that is now covered in piles. So you might take each pile you've made, store it in a clear plastic bag, and staple a label to the bag. Once you start the process again the next day (or in rare-but-acceptable cases, two weeks later), you'll know exactly what you're dealing with and won't have to wonder if that was the Alterations pile or the Try On pile. You dig?

ADDITIONAL CATEGORIES

Beyond the basics, you may start such piles as:

- **Bring to Work**
- **Return to Mom**
- **Maybe***

Whichever ones make sense for YOU.

*MAYBES ARE OK.

Throughout the process, there might be items that are difficult to make a decision about. Even using the purging criteria on pages 9–10 as a guide, you're a human who is allowed to be unsure. So *to keep things moving*, you can have a Maybe pile. However, after a few hours of sorting and purging, here's what usually happens: my clients look back through the Maybe pile and decide that about 95% of it can be donated or otherwise released from their lives. Reclaim what you really *need* and call it a day.

REAL LIFE

Look, it's A-OK to keep memorabilia. I wouldn't dare give up the 1970s rainbow mug I inherited from Mom and Dad. But it's one mug. Not eleven. And I ultimately wouldn't be shattered if *it* shattered. Because, while I love it and what it represents . . . it's just a mug.

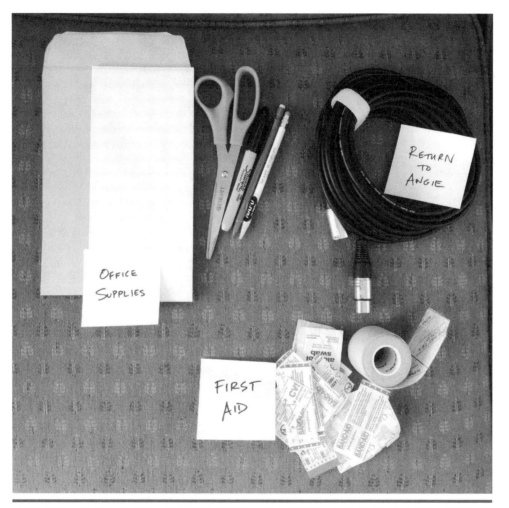

YOUR SORTED KEEPERS MIGHT LOOK LIKE THIS

PRO TIP

On the fence about purging certain memorabilia items? Take a photo. Back up that photo. Let go of the item(s). And parents, listen up: there are apps that can take the worry and stress out of "How much of my kid's artwork do I keep?!" Check out the resource list on page 173.

Everything you touched should now be in a labeled bin or pile. In chapter 2, we'll take the next *imperative* steps: getting rid of all the stuff you're ready to part with and deciding on new homes for your beloved Keepers.

Decluttering time should end with: delivering items that belong in Other Rooms, reassessing the Maybes, bringing donations out to the car (or close to the front door if you live car-free), and taking the trash out to the curb.

Okay. Now forget *everything* you just learned. You don't actually need any of these guidelines to make a real change. Walk around your space with the goal of getting rid of ten things. Stick 'em in a bag and then go donate, trash, or recycle them. It can be that easy.

2

LESS "WHERE THE F*&K IS IT?!"

DEAL WITH WHAT'S LEFT

You've sorted. You've let go. And sure, you're still staring at a bunch of stuff, but there's *less* of it than before. (Better, right?) AND you know *exactly* what you have left. (Better still.) Now is when we put it all back together—and get those donations and other discards out of your life for good.

One of the top queries I get from clients is, "Where's the *right* place to store it?" But the real question we want to be able to answer down the line is, "Where IS it??" (And "Can I access it ASAP?") It's not about what's right. It's about what's logical. Thus, my guiding principle for everyday items is to store things *where you use them*. So put *that* in your pipe, and read on.

If you're a writer, a musician, a visual artist, or any-one who often needs to sketch out or make note of spontaneous ideas, it's okay to have pen-and-pencil stations in as many places as you want. (I have five stations in one very small home.) Help yourself out. There's a big difference between "scattered around" and placed deliberately.

HOMES + CONTAINERS

Hopefully by purging all the stuff you don't need in any given area, you've already freed up some shiny new empty space. So in most cases, it'll be clear where Keeper items can live. Otherwise, just pick a place and try it out. The following section will help you narrow your options.

REAL LIFE

For years, I lived in a studio apartment with almost no cabinet space, so I stored my paper plates and cups in the freezer. There was a lot of unused real estate in there, and that's what worked for me.

Be a storage weirdo. It's cool.

MAKE IT ACCESSIBLE:
PRIME REAL ESTATE VS. HARD-TO-REACH AREAS

Your everyday items should get the good geography: easy-to-reach shelves, the fronts of drawers, the wall hooks that you're going to hang up next to the front door.

For the stuff you touch only now and then: high shelves and places you need a step stool to reach; the backs of cabinets; the garage or basement.

You don't have to fill up all of your space(s). For deep cabinets that stretch back into a black hole, try storing stuff only in the front.

Got a lotta drawers? Be an outlaw. Leave one empty. Leave room to breeeeeeeathe.

CONTAIN YOUR KEEPERS

For some of the Keepers, you might need new containers. It's not just "Where do I put it?" but "What do I put it *in* before I put it where I put it?"

Containers should be incredibly easy to open, close, take out, and put away. **An old-yet-sturdy shoe box with a snug-fitting lid is ten times better than a warped plastic tub that you paid too much money for five years ago.** (P.S. Get rid of that tub.)

Containerizing should go something like this: *I've got thiiiiis many music cables. Let me see what I have for them to live in. Here's an old milk crate that can fit under the bottom shelf in the hall closet. Done! OR Hmmm, can't find anything. I'll take a rough measurement to see how big of a container I'll need, and add "container for music cables, approx milk crate size" to the shopping list. Shop. Contain. Done!*

Shop in Your Home: Stuff You May Already Own and Its Potential Uses

- **Shoe boxes** (blank cards, old letters, overflow office supplies, first aid)
- **Small shipping boxes** (camping kit, wigs for dress-up, music cables, emergency supplies)
- **Bowls and cups** (your keys, writing utensils, toothbrushes)
- **Tupperware-like containers** (small sewing kit, extraneous art supplies)
- **Checkbook boxes, jewelry boxes, iPhone boxes** (dividers inside "junk" drawers)
- **Ziploc bags** (electronic wires for specific products, loose batteries)

The list of repurposed container ideas and uses is much longer than this, but you get the picture. Get creative with that space of yours. Think outside the container!

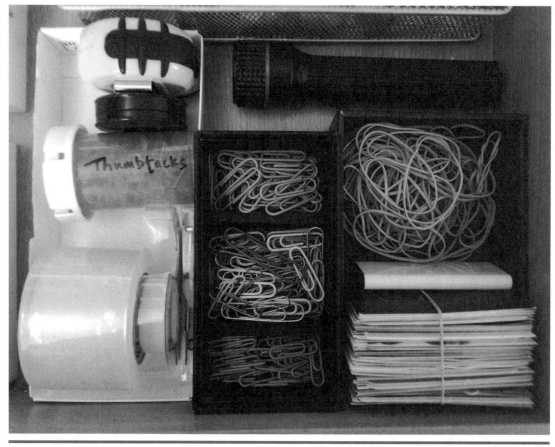

A "JUNK" DRAWER MADE BETTER BY USING A CHECKBOOK BOX, AN IPHONE BOX, AND A JEWELRY BOX AS DRAWER DIVIDERS. BOOM.

WHY WAIT TO SHOP?

Scenario 1: I have a cluttered pantry and feel overwhelmed. I buy a bunch of containers that look cool and say they can store nuts, grains, and cereals. I've now spent $250, I have even *more* stuff in my house, and I actually had more quinoa than I thought, so the size/quantity ratio is off. The project becomes even more paralyzing, so the new products get added to the hall closet with all the other unloved crap.

Scenario 2: I've spent three fruitful hours clearing out expired foods and making decisions about the pantry items I love to eat. At the end of this process I can see that two medium-size containers and two large ones should do the trick. I go to the store (or website) and spend $40 on *exactly what I need*.

I'm going to assume you can see that scenario 2 is the ideal. Life will be more enjoyable and satisfying this way. There will be less clutter this way. And you will **SAVE DOLLA BILLS.**

BUYING PRODUCTS

While official organizing products are the last stop (and sometimes the last resort), here are a few of my faves:

- **Wall shelves:** Regular ol' shelves that you drill into the wall. Still the best thing going. Can be as simple as a wood plank, a few brackets, and some anchored screws.
- **Hooks:** Regular ol' hooks. Like from the hardware store. Probably the most inexpensive and effective thing on this list. Great in a bedroom or entryway.
- **Undershelves (or undershelf baskets):** These slide onto standard-size shelves and immediately create another shelf beneath. One of The. Best. Ways. To maximize vertical space.
- **Small trays:** If you have a defined space for any given group of items, (a) it'll look nice *and* (b) you'll instantly know when it's time to declutter. Place on a desk, on a bathroom counter, or in an entryway.
- **Archive-safe boxes:** For art, photos, memorabilia, and valuable old documents. These boxes will protect them for years and years and years to come.

PRO TIP

It's cool if you simply like pretty things. (I do, too.) So if, after you've purged, you'd like to go a step beyond functionality and buy products that are also aesthetically pleasing and colorful, go for it. For visual folks, aesthetics can go a very long way in creating a space you love.

LABEL YOUR CONTAINERS

Labels are about *making it easier* on yourself. That's all. They don't have to represent rigidity or formality if those things aren't *your thing*. They're simply about knowing exactly what something is—immediately. You'll save yourself from buying items you already have if you can quickly open a cabinet and see that there are extra rolls of tape in a shoe box marked "extra rolls of tape."

If you've got containers stacked on top of other containers (which is not ideal but can be fine, depending on the access you need to each), you don't want to waste time lifting them all up, peeking inside, and taking inventory. You *think* you're going to remember what's inside. But it's *easier* to let the label remember for you.

There are labeling exceptions. You've always used that vintage orange suitcase to store old letters from college. You know that that's what's inside it. You'd never in a million years forget, because it's so dear to you. Great. No label necessary. And of course no labels are needed for things like "silverware drawer" and "guitar" on the outside of a guitar-shaped case. But go crazy if you want. (Just run it by whomever you share the space with.)

LABEL THEM HOW?

Five Options for Making Labels

1. An actual label maker.
2. Permanent marker on masking tape.
3. Permanent marker on paper, attached with tape.
4. Permanent marker on the container itself.
5. Anything, as long as you can easily read it.

Whatever works for you, dear reader.

Am I in deep love with my label maker? Of course I am—I'm a *professional organizer.* But let me just say: my clients are in deep love with my label maker, too. Regular folks like you, who once considered themselves "disorganized" and "not label-maker people," turn into geeks for labels as soon as these are applied within their own homes. I see it all the time. So if you feel like joining the club, I approve. (Personally, I prefer the ones with the QWERTY keyboards. Quicker typing.)

Permanent marker is a labeling god as well. Make no mistake.

PRO TIP

If you're labeling a rectangular box or container, label one short side *and* one long side. That way, no matter which way it fits best within a given space, you'll always be able to see the label.

GUITAR ACCESSORIES

- BATTERIES
- PRINTER INK
- TEA LIGHTS

WHEN CHOOSING LABEL NAMES, BE SPECIFIC.

This specificity goes for moving boxes, too. No more arriving at your new home to general words like "Dining Room" or "Office." *Write out what's inside.*

DONATE + DISPOSE

The trick is to get rid of donations ASAP. If you have a car, put them in the car. Do it now. Then choose a date on your calendar—maybe today?!—to actually take them to the drop-off donation center. (Don't know where the closest one is? Google it. Google it now.) Get into the habit of letting go of items on a regular basis by keeping a permanent Donate box near your front door or in a hall closet. The drop-offs are usually so so so easy, and the feeling you get from the new empty space is like being tipsy. On life.

Donating furniture or have too much awkward stuff to fit in the car? Or don't use a car? There are people and companies who will come to *you*. Flip to chapter 5 for a list.

Are you decluttering with such speed and grace that your home's or building's receptacles can't handle the amount of trash and recycling? Find out where the town dump is, and go there. Or ask a neighborhood business if you can chuck a few things in their dumpster. If necessary, *rent* a dumpster, or call a trash-hauling company. For everything you need, there is a service out there that will help you make it happen. **Be someone who makes it happen.**

PRO TIP

You can recycle old electronics or batteries for free at most big chain stores: Staples, Best Buy, Lowe's, Home Depot . . . the list goes on and on. See chapter 5 for specifics.

WHAT ABOUT SELLING?

I have only one question for you: **Are you really going to do it?**

Can you make some serious cash selling off your belongings? Maybe! Neat sites like Lifehacker always have great recommendations for how to get started—and it's a wonderful idea *if you're truly going to follow through.*

Here's what I see a lot of: piles of stuff that good folks *intend* to sell, via either Craigslist, eBay, or a local vendor. And they just . . . never get around to it. So the piles hang out. And guess what? Those piles aren't making any cash. They're sitting there, staring at you, bumming you out. And in the meantime, nobody gets to make use of the *stuff*!

This doesn't mean you're lazy or unmotivated, just that you're a busy person, and it's best to be realistic if you probably won't find the time to do it. I've said it before, and I'll say it again: decluttering your space is something your more joyous life depends on. Making an extra $30 is not. (If your current financial situation requires selling every last thing, there ain't no shame in that. Again: *if you're going to do it.*)

Therefore, my controversial recommendation is this:

If an item's value is less than $200 (not what you think **it's worth, but what you would** easily **make selling it), then donate it.** Get it out. Be done with it. Get on with your rad life.

If you haven't sold that $200-plus item in three months, donate it. And don't forget: donations = tax write-offs! (But more on that in chapter 5.)

You must weigh the cost of the time it'll take you to actually sell the thing. Consider taking nicely lit photos, driving it somewhere, coordinating with sellers, continuously checking the posting, etc. etc. etc. Instead, you're allowed to just **let it go.** You're certainly not making any money back by holding on to it (and not using it) all these years. So let someone else use it, out of the sheer goodness of your heart. And move the F on, friend.

MOVING ON

Guess what? It'll never all be done. Acceptance of this truth can be the most liberating thing in the world. Tomorrow or a month from now, more purchases will come through the door, more dishes will get dirty, and more laundry will need washing. Remember: **This work isn't about making your space magazine-perfect all the time.** (You'd gasp if you saw my place on a daily basis.) It's about choosing homes for your cherished belongings and being in better control of what's yours. It's about knowing when it's time to let go, and making donation trips a regular habit. It's about getting back to zero and delighting in *beginning again*. It's about getting high on the thrill of having *less*, and seeing what astonishing things are possible with an emptier space.

Later, we'll dig a little deeper into how to make decluttering an ongoing adventure. For now, if you can start to curb the consumption and accumulation of *new* stuff, you'll be doing yourself a huge favor and saving a lot of time and grief later on. Check in with yourself while you're in the store or about to click Buy:

- **Do I truly love or need it?**

- **Is it just another *thing* I'm largely indifferent to?**

- **Is it only in my cart because it's on sale?**

- **Do I actually have the room to store it?**

You get the idea.

FOR NEW STUFF THAT *DOES* MAKE THE CUT . . .

Discard packaging as quickly as possible.
If you know you're keeping it, take off the plastic, trim the tags, and make it as easy as possible to use when the time comes. This applies to dry-cleaning bags, too.

Empty your bags.
Empty both shopping and personal bags when you walk in the door. I cannot count the number of times I've gone through a neglected purse or suitcase

with a client and they remark, "*That's* where that is! I just bought a new one." From sweatshirts to vitamins to everything else, you've got stuff hiding out in the bottoms of bags. Stuff you don't want to have to buy again, stuff you might be using if you knew where it was. Go get empty.

Choose new homes. Be flexible.
If a new category of stuff comes into the house—supplies for a pottery class, extra paint for the family-room renovation—choose a new home for it. Simple. If it's hard to find room, make room by getting rid of something you don't need anymore. There will *always* be something you don't need anymore. Label new items to help remind your brain where they are. If you really wanna ace the test (this isn't a test!), download an app like Home Inventory and majorly geek out on what you own and where things are stored.

Go easy on yourself. Be gentle. Be imperfect. You're human. You make mistakes. I make mistakes. Sometimes the homes you chose for your stuff don't work anymore. Sometimes you have a new baby and your office turns into a nursery. Sometimes you move or start school or switch jobs. Life changes. Change with it. And remember that as long as it works for you, the only "right" place to store something is anywhere you want.

LESS PAPER

EASY-AS-PIE FILING + PAPER FLOW

For many of us, paper is taking up so much space in our homes and offices that it should be paying rent. What could you do with that space *instead*? Set up an easel or a didgeridoo station? Yeah—you could! Contrary to what it might feel like, those 8.5 x 11 suckers do not own you. And inch by inch, your reign over *them* is about to begin.

Paper is a different beast than Stuff. Decluttering it requires dedicated attention and the added task of, well, *reading*. So, for large piles, set aside some dedicated Paper Time that's separate from Stuff Time.

QUESTION:
How do you CREATE with a messy desk?

ANSWER:
Not as awesomely as you could.

Even for those of you who claim you "work better in chaos," you still need your *actual workspace* to be clear. You can't paint on top of a pile of papers, after all. So listen up.

For whatever you might be creating at your desk or in your workspace— a novel, a visual art piece, a Keynote presentation on the history of tango— you'll benefit from a little room to spread out and breathe. You don't want those messy piles giving you the evil eye and pulling your focus.

YOUR WORKSPACE = CURRENT PROJECTS AND BASIC TOOLS ONLY.
Everything else gets a new home (or is cast off forever).

In the same way you choose homes for your stuff, you must choose homes for your paper. And different types of paper will have different types of homes.

PAPER HOMES

The Basics

1. The papers you need to keep **for reference only** will primarily live in a hanging-file system: medical records, apartment lease, sentimental cards you've received.

2. You might store topical, informational paper on a corkboard or fridge for **quick reference:** class schedules, wedding invitations.

3. The papers you need to **take action on** will live in one of several temporary homes, or "middlemen," along the way: parking tickets to pay, forms to fill out, a monologue you're learning for class. These to-dos should be **in view** as opposed to hidden away in a file drawer.

With clients, I usually start by sorting and purging the paper that's staring us in the face (unopened mail, piles on the desk and dining-room table, etc.). We're simultaneously setting up a shiny new filing system that can be used for years to come. This process immediately attacks two all-important goals:

1. Getting rid of the papers you *don't* need.
2. Knowing exactly where to find the papers you do need.

SORTING + PURGING + SETTING UP FILES

You need files. Not a *ton* of files. But some. Files are not just for businesses or 9-to-5ers. They're for all of us. We all use paper and we all get mail and we all pay taxes. So we all need files. (Later we'll talk about steps toward going paperless. But for now, let's live in the physical world.)

If your old files are in disarray but the thought of touching them feels paralyzing, better to start a brand-new set of files that will work *from now on.* I'd rather you have duplicate file categories than a pile of crap on your desk.

THE PREP

Soooo . . . I know I opened this book by telling you not to go buy products. And I meant it. However, the one and only time to have specific organizing products on hand—if you don't already—is when dealing with paper.

SHOPPING LIST
(UNDER 30 BUCKS, Y'ALL!)

1. **File crate or desktop file box** that can accommodate letter-size files.* Must be designed for hanging files with those grooves that files can rest on.

2. **Letter-size hanging files.** A standard box of 25 should get you started real nice. Get all one color—choose a shade that makes you smile.

3. **3x3 yellow Post-it notes.** Grab the Super Sticky ones. Worth it.

4. **Bonus: letter opener.** Makes opening mail a breezier process. For a dollar.

*When using a crate or box for files, I prefer the ones without lids. Why? Because if you have the ability to shut your files away, you will. And the likelihood of the system breaking down over time increases if you have any barriers to filing things easily and quickly. To that end, **DO NOT PUT ANY- THING ON TOP OF YOUR FILES. EVER EVER.** (If you prefer a file cabinet or file drawer, do not ever block the drawers. Please. And thank you.)

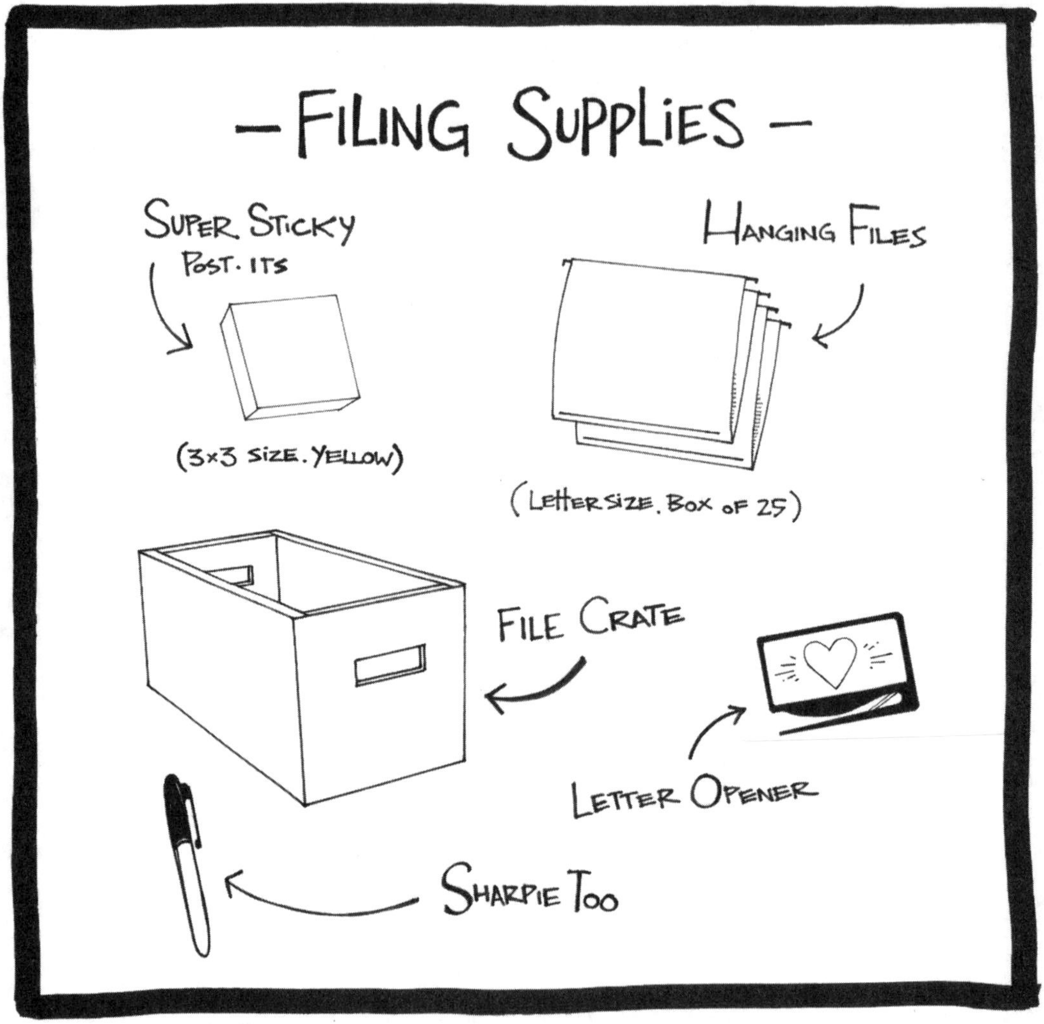

— FILING SUPPLIES —

SUPER STICKY
POST·ITS

(3×3 SIZE. YELLOW)

HANGING FILES

(LETTER SIZE. BOX OF 25)

FILE CRATE

LETTER OPENER

SHARPIE TOO

Accordion files kinda suck for your regular files. They get bulky and keep things hidden away.

Get a file crate or solid file box instead.

Once your supplies are ready to go, clear a space and get out your Recycle and Shred bins. (If you happened to skip chapter 1, I explained how beneficial it is to have simple, labeled receptacles for each discard category. See illustration, page 4.) With paper, the discards are usually just Recycle or Shred, but if you've got large piles of magazines (back issues of *The New Yorker*, anyone?) that you'd like to donate to a doc's office or library, create a Donate bin as well. Don't use the floor for discards . . . you'll save yourself from a headache later.

Open up your box of folders and hang 'em in the file box. Have Post-its and Sharpie at the ready, plus your letter opener to zip through any envelopes.

Gather the most pressing papers first—items that either most require your attention or are most in your way. The amount you gather doesn't need to be more than a few inches high for now. Start small if that feels right.

THE MAIN EVENT

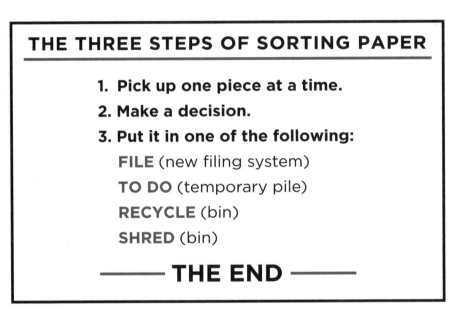

THE THREE STEPS OF SORTING PAPER

1. **Pick up one piece at a time.**
2. **Make a decision.**
3. **Put it in one of the following:**
   FILE (new filing system)
   TO DO (temporary pile)
   RECYCLE (bin)
   SHRED (bin)

—— THE END ——

Have no fear. For most items, the choices will be extremely easy.

If paper is a Keeper and does NOT require action, make a file for it. To keep things *click-clacking* along, use an upside-down Post-it as a temporary tab and stick it on the inside of a folder with the label sticking out. Place the paper inside. You can make proper tabs later.

Quicker than you can say *procrastination*, your new files will be growing before your eyes. **Choose the first folder names that come to you right now, and don't worry about the order.** Just get going. It'll look like this:

WORK CONTRACTS

MEMORABILIA

PARENTS

APARTMENT
(Lease + Notices)

HEALTH INSURANCE

CAR INSURANCE

PAY STUBS

CHECKING ACCT.

PRO TIP

IMPORTANT PAPERS

You'll find an array of opinions on what to keep and what to toss. I actually err on the cautious side with important papers. A quick Google search for "what papers to keep" will bring up several solid lists of Keepers and shredders. Here's my down-n-dirty version, based on what people ask me the most:

1. Tax returns = forever

2. Birth certificates, wills, etc. = forever (ideally in a fireproof safe or safety deposit box)

3. Deductible receipts (expenses related to your biz / your craft) = ten years*

Everything else: check with your tax pro. **If it feels important, keep it.**

*Disclaimer: This is *my* round-number preference. Do check with your tax professional for final say. Thank you so much.

If you come across old records, like 1099s from a long-ago job, make a temporary file. Later on, you might reuse (or purchase) a Bankers Box for out-of-the-way, long-term storage. Label one long side and one short side, something simple, like "TAXES 2011 + 2012." (You can also have a separate box or file that is ONLY your tax *returns*, as those you'll keep forever.)

If a piece of paper is a Keeper and DOES require action, make a dedicated To Do pile off to the side, which you'll deal with after you finish sorting and filing.

With the exception of very quick tasks (e.g., inputting one address into your phone contacts and then trashing the paper it's written on), don't start to *do* your to-dos during this process or you'll never finish the task at hand—which is paring down your paper and creating a working file system.

When it comes to making choices about unnecessary paper, be honest with yourself.

REAL LIFE

Are you really gonna create that recipe binder you've always dreamed of? If so, grrreat. Get it *done* within 30 days or recycle all those printed-out recipes and use your computer or iPad instead.

Life's too short for dawdling.

WHAT TO SHRED

I shred nearly everything personal and business-related, which reaches far beyond social security and account numbers. But some experts say there's not much to worry about—these days, identity thieves are more likely to use the Internet rather than dig through your trash. **Do what feels comfortable for you. And when in doubt: shred.**

To stay on top of the task, designate an area to throw shredables as they come to you—a small bin under your desk, maybe. Then every week you can shred pages in digestible amounts.

If you don't own a shredder, you have three choices:

1. Take your paper to a local company that will do it for you. (Or maybe you can sneak it in at work. Please don't hold me responsible if you get in trouble.)
2. Rip everything up to your own satisfaction and put it in the recycle bin.
3. Buy a shredder—and use it. Don't go with the cheapest models, which are more likely to break down over time. Go at least one level up, and keep it tucked away but accessible.

PUT A TAB ON IT

Save the last 20 minutes of your sorting and purging time to make some lasting labels. Use the tabs that came with your box of folders to write out category names. (Say farewell to your temporary Post-its and recycle them or make some tiny origami.) You can attach a tab to either the front *or* the back of a folder. (Oh, the freedom!) It's up to you—as long as it's uniform.

Choose the names that make the most sense to you. Perhaps you found some Car paperwork, but then later you found some Car *Insurance* paperwork that you'd like kept separate from the other stuff. So you might change the first category to Car Repair + DMV. Yeah? Don't be too precious about the naming. Keep it simple but specific. There are no right or wrong names, and you can always change something later.

Handwriting, as long as it's legible, is FINE. If you're finding your desired words aren't fitting on the tabs and you wanna get craaaaazy, buy a set of ⅓-cut tabs for your hanging folders. They're longer, and thus can fit more text. (And, of course, if you joined the label-maker club in chapter 2, do it up.)

Now feel free to choose an order for your files. **Organize by importance and usability, placing the most-accessed categories toward the front. Or order them alphabetically.** Whatever works best for you is the right way to go.

STRAIGHT-LINE FILING

A term originally coined by the fine folks at Smead (they make folders), straight-line filing is a process of putting all the tabs in the same place along the tops of all your folders. And I highly recommend it. So instead of left, center, and right tabs, your tabs would *all* be on the right, for instance. There are two primary reasons for doing it this way:

1. Our eyes (and thus our brains) function better when they're required to look in only one single direction, instead of jetting around to three possible areas. We can find something faster when we know exactly where to look.

2. Life changes fast, which means you'll probably need to add or subtract a folder once in a while. This would bring immediate upset to a left-center-right system and cause your files to look (and therefore *feel*) cluttered.

Seeeee?

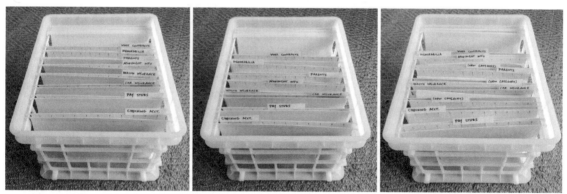

Set up files like THIS   **Instead of like THIS**   **So that over time, the tabs don't end up like THIS**

One add-on option: place tabs for larger categories on the opposite side, to delineate different sections of files. Check it out to the right.

And TA-DA! Your new filing system is born. Later on, if you'd like to *merge* any old files you have with these new ones—after a proper purge of the old ones, of course—then keep the party going! In fact, I call this the Purge 'n Merge. Use the same techniques to discard old papers you no longer need, and then add any Keepers to your new filing system. By now, you're an expert.

PRO TIP

Keep some empty folders hanging out with your filing system, and make new files as soon as new categories come through the door. Your kid just started karate lessons. Make a Karate folder. Even if it's only with a Post-it for now! This one-minute task will keep heaps of paper clutter at bay.

WHERE TO KEEP YOUR FILES

It's up to you if you'd like to use filing cabinets. But you don't *need* anything so formal. In clients' homes, I've placed filing crates everywhere from low kitchen cabinets to the floor of a hall closet. **The key is easy, everyday access to quickly slip in papers you need to keep.** For the archival tax papers, apply the storage principles from chapter 2. Because you need to access that stuff only about once a year, it can be stored on high shelves or in a basement or attic. While you don't want to have to move a lot of stuff out of the way to access it when the time comes, you also don't want it cluttering up your daily life.

THOSE TO-DOS

You've probably set aside several items that need attending to—like, ASAP. Keep your overwhelm in check by remembering the "small steps" mantra. The reality is: you have to deal with these things no matter what. At least now you know where the papers are! Next you'll learn how to choose a more permanent home for these action-oriented papers, and in chapter 6 you'll learn how to start *writing down* your to-dos in a trusted place.

Welcome to Adulthood.

ENLIST MIDDLEMEN

To-dos need a home while waiting *to be done.* A home that's *not* your kitchen table, your couch, or the ever-growing pile on your desk. There can be a *chain* of homes, in fact, that your paper lives in before its final resting place. **These temporary homes are called "middlemen."** And I don't care how many middlemen you have if the system works for you.

For instance, you might have a wall file that houses incoming mail as soon as you've opened it. Once that wall file is full, you bring mail to the table to process it.

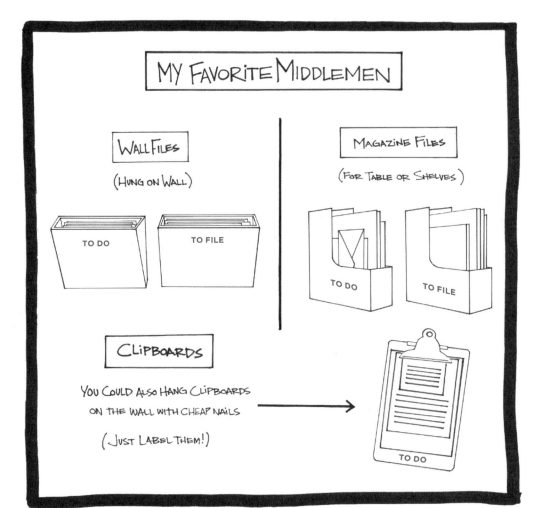

Possible Middlemen Categories

- Incoming Mail
- To Read
- To Pay
- To File
- Shred
- Show My Wife
- Send to CPA
- Current Projects
- Whatever you want

Your middlemen shouldn't be too big. The reason I love magazine files and wall files so much is that they set a realistic limit on how much can fit, and thus they must be dealt with in bite-size helpings. No big baskets or magazine *racks* . . . forbidden. "But one day's worth of mail would fill up a whole huge basket," you say. "Then you need to get less mail," I say. And we're about to get to that.

PRO TIP

Stacking trays are where papers go to die. Whenever anything covers anything else, you run a high risk of "out-of-sight, out-of-mind" syndrome. Plus, it's challenging to keep stacking-tray labels in clear view. I suggest they be used for **blank paper only.**

For some, having middlemen will seem like a dream come true. For others, it may overcomplicate. So while you're allowed to have as many categories as works for you, it's certainly not a requirement. **I have only three: To Do Urgent, To Do When I Can, and To File.** (And everything hanging out in the To Do Urgent area is also *a written task* on my to-do list. See chapter 6.)

Trust your instincts. And spread the word. "Hey, honey, let's try putting our mail here, and only here, every day. After we read it, it can go in this *very clearly marked* wall file and get HANDLED." Commit to the experiment and see what happens.

If you have a clear chain of middlemen, you won't lose papers. Period.

Day-to-Day Protocol: OPEN YOUR MAIL.

For all the *new* paper that enters your life, cut clutter off at the pass.

Your first line of defense against paper clutter is to open mail as soon as it comes in the door.

This doesn't mean you have to *deal* with it then. Simply *open* it and discard the detritus. (If someone else brings in the mail, open yours when *you* walk through the door.)

You may be saying: "But I have to start making dinner as soon as I get home." "Other people are asking things of me." "I'm too tired . . ."

And here's what *I'm* saying: THIRTY. SECONDS.

Start the habit. On a daily basis. (And then, of course, deviate from your new norm at those times when you're left holding the proverbial baby. Or an actual baby.)

Here's what those 30 seconds look like:

1. Use your (new) letter opener to quickly open everything.

2. Recycle envelopes, packaging, inserts, junk mail, and any catalogs or magazines that you know you won't read. (Be brutal.)

THE TOOLS THAT WILL MAKE IT 1,000X EASIER

1. That letter-opener *stationed* in your entryway. (Seriously, it'll be the best $1–$2 you spend maybe ever.) Put it on a side table. Velcro it to a wall. Just make sure it's there.

2. Permanent Recycle and Shred bins in your entryway, too. They can be very small receptacles that you empty each week. (They can also be good-looking, if aesthetics are a factor for you.) If you have no entryway, make sure those bins live somewhere easy to toss discards into, each and every day.

As soon as you've opened the mail, paper can be dropped into the afore-mentioned Incoming Mail middleman near the door. Or it can go straight into a more specific middleman (e.g., To Pay). Aaaaaand . . . piles avoided.

That's IT. Congrats! In trying out this new, seconds-long habit, you've just saved yourself future hours, days, eons . . .

PRO TIP

If you're trying to get significant others on board with new habits but they're resistant to the cause, forcing them into it is usually futile. The most effective way to create happy change? Clean up your own side of the street, and gracefully lead by example. I've seen this work wonders for more than a couple o' couples.

LESS MAIL

Of course, another all-important way to have less paper is to *receive less mail*. And the first step is to avoid the junk in the first place. Two companies that ace junk mail are Catalog Choice and PaperKarma. Use their fine services to get off mailing lists in record time. (Flip to "Apps, Websites + Additional Resources" at the end of this book for more list-removal sites.)

But it's not just about canceling the junk mail you *know* you don't want. It's about reassessing which once-desired items you still need to be getting in the first place.

FEWER CATALOGS AND MAGAZINES

Even if the catalogs are from your favorite store, are they piling up and spilling over? Adding to the bulk of the never-ending mail? Can you get your info online instead? And what if you, *gulp,* **shopped less**? As for the magazines—are you actually reading them? What do they provide for you? Call it out. How do they make you feeeeel?

If you *aren't* finding the time to read everything you subscribe to, it's possible you keep it hanging around because you think, "If I don't read it, I might be missing something! Something important and life-changing!" Or: "One of these days, I'm going to take these back issues to the beach and rip through them all." This becomes an unconscious and never-ending thought pattern that leaves us feeling inadequate. Friends: We only have so much time on this planet. Stop spending that time allowing the paper to torture you. **You're not missing anything. Life is right in front of you.**

Either start reading your mags or cancel your subscriptions. (And so what if you don't get a refund. Your peace of mind is worth a lot more than 20 bucks.)

If you're scared of letting go of something you *have* **read, remember: on the Internet you can pull up nearly every article ever written in no time.** If the article is a true Keeper, snap a photo or scan it into an appropriately named digital folder or Evernote notebook. (A bit more on scanning in a minute.) If the article happens to be *about* you or a loved one, feel free to also keep a physical copy in a labeled archive-safe memorabilia box. But in most cases, be free of the paper and let it go.

(And if you're part of the small population that still gets the newspaper delivered—and reads it—then keep on doing what you're doing. I salute you. Just *recycle* it when you're done, please.)

FEWER BILLS

Are you still writing checks for every monthly bill? I'm afraid that'll have to stop. **Online Bill Pay has a spot at the table for you.** Go to your bank's website, log in to your account, and follow the prompts that'll allow you to easily pay your cable, Internet, gas, and other bills online every month, either manually or by auto-pay. While you're at it, **opt in to paperless billing, too**. Most, if not all, of your providers will send statements by email instead. Go ahead, you can figure it out. That 30 to 60 minutes now will save you hours upon hours of opening mail and writing checks for the rest of your life.

Maybe you *haven't* done this already because you're afraid you'll miss something if it doesn't show up at your door. Understandable, especially if your email inbox is all cluttered up and/or you don't have a trusted to-do list. Chapters 4 and 6 can help you out with those two things, respectively. And then, little by little, you can learn to trust a system that helps you tackle all your paper-related tasks—without the actual paper.

If you're deducting any monthly bills as business expenses, make sure the charges are showing up on your bank and/or credit card statements, and you should be good to go for tax purposes[2]. If you need the itemized bills, set your-

---

[2] Again, kindly check with your tax pro for final say.

self a reminder to download PDFs from the companies' websites every three months. Save them to a computer folder marked "Bills [+ current year]." (Then back it up.) That 15 minutes will be considerably less time than it will take to open up all that mail throughout the year. But check it: there are free apps like FileThis that will do all that downloading *for you*.

You're allowed to keep getting paper statements for any accounts you feel precious about. If that makes you feel more comfortable, so be it. But those electricity bills? Nope.

PRO TIP

Speaking of bills and expenses, I use Mint to track all my spending. It puts all my account balances in one place and adds up my various deductions for me in real time. For further budgeting advice, I enjoy a blog called Our Freaking Budget. They've got resources galore, plus they're hilarious.

GOING FURTHER: PAPERLESS + SCANNING

Paperless billing is a sensational start. But you may consider going even further, by digitizing almost ALL of the paper that's in your life. Essentially turning that filing system we made into an all-digital cabinet. (And holding on to *only* the bare essentials in physical form.)

For some folks, going paperless can start immediately. If you are really feeling the momentum, start scanning your Keeper documents right after you've sorted and purged. Make sure you save them as PDFs and give them descriptive document names, using dates and a uniform system for collections of similar documents. Place those documents within corresponding digital folders, e.g., "2016_05_21_WeddingContract_Miller.pdf" inside the "Wedding Photography Contracts" folder. *And back up your data.* (More on that in chapter 4.) Going paperless need not be some huge mountain to climb. And if you don't have a scanner, smartphones scan, too. I use Evernote's Scannable app to take surprisingly high-quality scans of documents and business cards. **The key is being able to find it later when you need it.**

PRO TIP

Two of the leading experts on "going paperless" are Brooks Duncan of DocumentSnap and David Sparks of MacSparky. They know way more than I do, and have created stellar resources for learning how to make going paperless a reality. Use them.

For others, going further will come later. If all this paper has been overwhelming you for months or yearrrrs, focus on the small steps. Congratulate yourself on getting started. Even if you *never* want to go entirely paperless, you're still a worthy being on earth.

Them's the basics, folks. Start with even a few things from this chapter, and you'll notice a huge difference in the day-to-day quality of your life. And by all means, know this:

Piles happen.

Even after setting yourself up for paper-flow greatness, you may sometimes come home to a messy pile on the kitchen table. It's normal.

But take heart: your clean-up time is now quick and painless because each piece of paper has a happy new home.

LESS DIGITAL

EMAILS + NOTIFICATIONS + SOCIAL MEDIA

We wake up each morning only to get promptly swallowed up by The Daily Avalanche of Everything. There is a shocking amount of *content* out there—emails to read, riveting blog posts, photos of what your camp friend ate for breakfast—and somehow we imagine ourselves capable of consuming every last bit. **If we can just get to *all of it*, then we'll be . . . cooler? Smarter? More complete?** Sigh. It's a futile thought process. (Well, I suppose you *could* read all the way to the bottom of the Twitter feed . . . Or you could play that guitar for 20 minutes.)

> "How we spend our days is, of course, how we spend our lives. What we do with this hour, and that one, is what we are doing."
>
> —ANNIE DILLARD

It's also a near impossibility to *refrain* from the cycle of consumption. Heck, I love a Pinterest board just as much as the next gal. So again, the path to Better . . . to a little more creative bliss . . . is to simply consume *less*.

DIGITAL CLUTTER

(THE DAILY AVALANCHE OF EVERYTHING)

Just imagine for a minute . . . If you spent less time dealing with digital distractions, what could you be doing instead? What do you *want* to make time for? What have you been putting off? Writing a short story . . . exploring . . . sleeping . . . learning a language . . . enjoying in-person human contact . . . touching a tree? The world is yours.

The first step to consuming less is to reassess our relationship with digital life.

- **What do we truly want from our tech-based connections?**

- **What parts are we willing to sacrifice for greater clarity?**

- **And what do we want (or not want) to be interrupted by? (Begone, push notifications and unwanted newsletters!)**

It's about getting conscious and then taking action that's *in line* with that consciousness.

You may think you have zero downtime, and perhaps you're right. But if you're struggling to plant that mini herb garden on the balcony *and* you're also aware of what your 27 favorite celebs are tweeting about at any given time of day, then the time *is* there, friend—you just gotta reclaim it.

DECLUTTERING YOUR EMAIL

Your email inbox is as messy as your clothes closet. Clear the clutter. Feel the flow.

What's your email inbox *for*? Well, these days it is the number one form of communication, period. It covers our personal and professional lives, and for the most part, we're expected to use it. The most effective and time-saving approaches involve clearing away the brush to move through it as swiftly as possible.

If you are a creative person who wants to get things done, it's imperative to have a handle on your email and communication. When I'm collaborating with fellow artists, their email etiquette tells me multitudes about whether we're in for a good working relationship. It's become my preference to work with kind and efficient communicators—those who reply in a timely manner and who keep replies short and sweet.

What's your current email inbox count? 300? 2,500ish? 48,716? Every-one has a threshold for how many emails feels overwhelming. And whatever your number is, you're not alone. It's incredibly common for smart people like you to have thousands upon thousands of emails living right on your phone. And if it doesn't bother you in the least, you're a lucky minority. But if you dream of a streamlined inbox, certain of the relief it would bring, these next steps are for you.

BE HONEST WITH (AND EASY ON) YOURSELF

Let's say you have 10,000 emails in your inbox. What are the chances you're going to go back and scroll through all 10,000 and respond to each one you missed? If you haven't done it by now, might you just forgive yourself and let the task go? Chances are, the consequences of removing these emails from your inbox will *not* be life-and-death. If someone really needs to contact you, they'll try again (perhaps through one of the other zillion means of communication we have available to us these days). And if you keep forgetting something important that's buried in there, you'll likely remember it again—and this time, you'll be ready.

START FRESH. ARCHIVE YOUR BACKLOG.

The quickest way to declutter your email inbox is to ARCHIVE everything that no longer needs dealing with. This means that if you have 10,000 emails but you know you'll only ever reply to the first 50, you can select all 10,000 in one move, deselect those 50 (manually, but that ain't so bad), click the Archive button, and immediately watch 9,950 emails disappear—instant slate-cleaning. (The best way to do this may differ from provider to provider, but you get the idea.)

Note that archiving is different from *deleting*. Right this second, I have 27 emails in my inbox. But over time I've archived about 24,000 more, all easily searchable if I ever want to bring something up from yesterday or seven years ago. They live in Gmail's All Mail folder. I pay Google $5 a year for a little extra storage, and it's worth it for my peace of mind. But I don't want to *see* all those emails every day. And I don't have to.

Hotmail now has a built-in archive as well. For email providers that don't, you can easily create specific folders and save your archival emails there.

UNSUBSCRIBE. FROM PRETTY MUCH EVERYTHING.

You bought one sweater three years ago from some random clothing company that now emails you newsletters five times a week. *Why should you stand for this?* I don't mean they're wrong to do it: they're running a business. But you don't deserve clutter that doesn't serve you: you're running a *life*. For the newsletters you *did* sign up for, once upon a time: How many of them are you actually reading? Are they analogous to that stack of magazines, taunting you with information that you don't have time for? **If you make them disappear, you can be free.** How? Every newsletter has a handy Unsubscribe link at the bottom, and Gmail and Hotmail now offer additional buttons for this purpose. To do some magical **mass-unsubscribing,** sign up for Unroll.Me or Mailstrom and prepare to be floored with amazement.

REAL LIFE

I've seen clients go from 30,000-plus emails to 20 in under a week. It's easier than you think. Just decide and do.

DAY-TO-DAY EMAIL PROTOCOLS

After decluttering the bulk of the beast, there are a few simple practices that can help you maintain that slimmed-down look and save time moving forward.

KEEP YOUR EMAILS SHORT

No more lengthy, drawn-out, overly apologetic emails. ("Sorry to bother you," "Sorry for the mass email," "Here's everything you ever wanted to know about this subject in only 18 short paragraphs.") You don't have time for this. And neither does your receiver. If you're writing a long letter to a friend or family member and *that's how you guys do,* fine. But get in the habit of editing. We're going for: short, efficient, and kind. And if you're finding that you're spending 45 minutes on one email, pick up the phone instead. No, not to text. To *make a call.*

PRO TIP

Bring phone calls back! I have spent hours of my life crafting the "perfect" email about something that could have been solved in a five-to-ten-minute call. Direct human contact is always quicker. Be brave. Save time. Use the telephone.

SEND LESS

Junk email isn't the only clutter culprit. The more email you send, the more you will receive. Sometimes I balk at this theory: "If people would only stop sending me so much crap . . ." I say. "It's not me, it's *them!*" And then every time I take a break from initiating emails, I have fewer emails to deal with. Without fail.

NO REPLY NECESSARY

Experiment with adding "No need to reply" to the end of your emails. The person at the other end will feel no guilt for the conversation being over, and you've saved *yourself* another reply to look at.

CHECK IT LESS

Perhaps a no-brainer, but bears repeating over and over because we are utterly addicted to checking our email. (Based on what I've observed in myself and my clients, many of us are refreshing that inbox well over a hundred times per day!) Choose a number of times per hour or day that feels more reasonable. Yes, make a rule. Otherwise, the constant checking is clutter itself. Let your brain breathe. Let your imagination run wild instead.

USE VACATION RESPONDERS

One of my writer friends uses an auto-responder whenever she's on a deadline, alerting everyone that they will not be hearing back from her via email. If it's urgent, they can use the telephone. Every time I receive it, I'm thrilled she's made a solid move toward more efficiency and less noise during her busy times. Some people turn on their vacation responders every day at 6:00 p.m., alerting senders that they ain't gettin' nothin' until the next morning. Still others *always* have theirs on, clearly stating that they check email only at certain times of day. What bliss.

STOP TREATING YOUR EMAIL INBOX LIKE A TO-DO LIST

While your inbox should be viewed as a trusted place for information and communication, it shouldn't be treated as storage for to-dos. In chapter 6, you'll learn more about transferring tasks to an ironclad to-do list—so that you can archive those emails instead.

SEND & ARCHIVE

If you use Gmail and you don't have the "Send & Archive" feature enabled—in which it does both simultaneously—please go to your settings and do it now. This is a game-changer for decluttering. If the email you're sending is the end of the conversation, or you know you'll get a needed reply back, you can swiftly kill two birds with one button. (While we're at it, enable the "Undo Send" feature in Gmail as well. Ever wished you could take back an email? You can. Just one more way to make technology work for *you*.)

USE AN APP THAT "BOOMERANGS" OR "PAUSES" YOUR EMAILS

The pièce de résistance for your less-cluttered inbox is the ability to choose when certain emails appear there. For example: It's Tuesday and you've been sent an email from your cousin, detailing his last adventurous vacation. You *want* to take the time to read it, but realistically you won't be able to until the weekend. You can make that email disappear from your inbox—and stop cluttering up your week—and have it return there on Saturday. This ability is the number one reason my daily inbox count stays low. The future is here! Robots exist! Let's use them. A few great ones: Mailbox, Boomerang for Gmail, Inbox Pause.

A FEW WORDS ON DIGITAL PHOTOS

Like paper, photos are their own friendly monster. And while your backlog may be pretty frightening, do apply the small-steps mantra here. Even if you don't organize all your *old* photos, you can start taking better care of the *new* ones. Temper that overwhelm. It's not all or nothing.

There's a photo guru out there named Cathi Nelson. She founded an organization called Association of Personal Photo Organizers, whose pros have a ton of tips to get you going, on both digital and physical photos. Check out appo.org for how-tos and resources.

In the meantime, and at the very least . . .

1. Back 'em up, wherever they are. Even if your photos are not particularly organized, make sure you know how to access them if your primary devices fail.

2. From now on, try not taking so many. And delete as you go. If we take 14 angles of a cheeseburger just because we can, we're our own clutter culprits. Need to get the right shot? Great. Once you've nailed it, delete, delete, delete.

Photos are for special times, not all the times.

SOCIAL MEDIA MINDFULNESS

Can your world be utterly changed for the better by your interactions with social media? Of course. Can you also have a fully realized, happy existence *without* a Facebook profile? Without a doubt. So let's go into this section agreeing that there are no rights or wrongs here. Different strokes for different folks. I myself have chosen to engage in a certain amount of the stuff, both for business and for pleasure. And when I know *why* I'm using it—sharing helpful info for my followers, having easy access to my friends' kids' cute faces, linking to my favorite bands' music videos—I'm a happier me. It's all about making social media interactions a choice rather than a passive activity or obligation. And then better policing that choice.

Somewhere in your gut, you know if you're spending too much time on social media, if that amount of time is truly serving you, and if there are other things that your soul is certain to be more fulfilled by.

TAKE SOCIAL MEDIA STOCK

What are your reasons for engaging with social media? Call them out. Promoting your creative projects or business? Connecting with old friends? Trying out comedy material? Reading the news? Get as specific as possible. Heck, spend five minutes writing it down. One great function of this call-out is that when you find you're in a social media spiral, you can ask yourself: Am I actively fulfilling one of these goals? Or am I wasting my damn time?

PARENT YOURSELF

"You're allowed to watch TV after you finish your homework and practice your viola." Those childhood rules worked. And without them, we might not have gotten diplomas or learned how to put on underwear. Many of us need rules and time limits for social media, too. This way, we're *consciously* giving ourselves time and freedom for life's other goodnesses . . . because it's never too late to learn the viola. Sites that do the parenting for you, by keeping you off certain *other* sites at the times you specify, include Anti-Social, Freedom, and SelfControl.

Schedule Your Posts

Artists and entrepreneurs need to promote. But it can be done in advance, in batches. There are people out there who *appear* to be online 24/7, but they're really not . . . surprise! If I have an upcoming gig, for instance, I use an app called Hootsuite to schedule 90% of my tweets about it weeks before the curtain actually goes up. Then when showtime nears, I can take a break from my devices, and maybe go for a head-clearing stroll instead.

HIDING PEEPS

You don't have to be social media buddies with everybody. And you do *not* have to keep seeing the same ol' posts you loathe. If you're not comfortable unfriending or unfollowing, some apps let you hide or mute people from your feeds. It's the equivalent of unsubscribing to stuff you don't need. Make a habit of it. (They'll never know!)

CONSIDER A HOLIDAY

If you feel like social media time may really be impeding on your happier life, consider a clean break. What's the worst that could happen if you disabled your

account(s) for a while? I recently spent almost two years with no personal Facebook profile. I didn't miss a thing. And my creative output was significant. Just saying.

TEXTS + IMS

The ability to text and instant-message people is *totallyfuckingbrilliant*. But who decided that we all have to respond right away, every time, no matter what we're doing? Let's collectively put an end to this absurdity. **Multitasking is a big enemy to productivity and creativity**. I bet 99% of the time, you do not need to be reachable within seconds. Where's the freedom in that? If you're working, writing, hiking, *living*, don't respond to those pings right away! Invite some breathing room into your life and gently teach others that you have an existence outside your devices. Come to think of it, a lot of those pings and dings should be silenced for the duration.

NOTIFICATIONS

Okay, so let me get this straight: You're on Facebook, Twitter, Pinterest, LinkedIn, Instagram, etc., etc., between 10 and 100 times per day. And on each site there are easy-to-see notifications you can read through when you're *there*. But you *also* get emails every time something happens on one of these sites? Oh—*and* a message pops up on your phone, too?!! And sometimes the notification is just to tell you that someone you don't even know has commented on a post about a baby llama that you also commented on???? I'm hoping that when I say it like this, it sounds as silly to you as it does to me . . . that it sounds like *obvious clutter*.

If there are posts from a few people you don't want to miss, it's understandable that you'd subscribe to their feeds. And just like those few magazines and newsletters you actually read and interact with, any notifications that are truly useful to you should be kept. HOWEVER . . . **turning off social media notifications = turning down the clutter. Way down.** Go to the Settings section on each site and on your smartphone. Your email inbox will thank you, and your brain will thank you.

LESS RISK

This section is not necessarily about how to have less stuff; it's about how to have less of a headache should anything happen to your devices or personal information. Headaches are unnecessary clutter, too.

It comes down to this: Back up your shit.

What I find with most clients is that they *know* they should be backing up their info, and they've heard of the services that do so. But they continue to put off pulling the trigger. Get real with yourself and ask: "Why?" Is it a fear that you won't know how to use the app the "right way"? Do you think you're immune to crashes? Are you not valuing the work or media on your computer that deserves to be safe? Whatever your reasoning, call it out. And then back it up. For god's sake.

The two simplest methods are:

1. Cloud backup
2. External hard drive

Programs like Backblaze and CrashPlan will back up your entire computer's contents to the cloud—automatically and continuously. It takes, I kid you not, less than five minutes to set up. For a hard backup (or if you're uncomfortable with your information being "in the cloud"), use a program like Apple's Time Machine to automatically back up your computer's contents to an external drive. Some people, including myself, use both methods.

There's no shame in seeking out the good people at the Apple store[3] or Googling any issues that come up during the process of setting up these programs—or any other. I've searched in more help forums than I can count. The resources are out there.

In addition to your primary computer backup, which stores the contents of your entire computer, there are programs like Apple's iCloud that—once activated—will help you sync and share your Apple-based applications and media (photos, contacts, calendar, etc.). For instance, say your phone battery has died and you're away from your computer. You'd like to retrieve a telephone number that's in your Contacts. If you had iCloud enabled for your Contacts, you'd be able to log in to iCloud.com from any device and find the digits you need.

Lastly: **Make friends with Dropbox.** For free, you get 2GB of storage space in the cloud. Dropbox is more of an application you use on a daily basis—not just a place to store and back up data, but a place to interact with that data and share it with others. In addition, Dropbox is a whiz at syncing your files to any device you're using. So it's not uncommon for people to use a backup program like the ones listed above, as well as Dropbox for everyday storage and flexibility across devices.

[3] I know, I'm Mac-leaning. But nearly every resource in this book works for all platforms.

PASSWORDS

I don't have to tell you why you need strong passwords. You've seen email and social media accounts hacked—perhaps your friends' or perhaps your own. And we've all heard news stories about sensitive info being retrieved from cloud services and phones. Turns out people are still using passwords like "Mom123." Sound familiar?

You are not immune to hacking. No one is. This doesn't mean don't use the Internet. It means use it wisely, and with strong passwords. So if you would hyperventilate if someone else had access to, say, your Twitter or Gmail (or bank!) accounts, it's time to take control. Within 30 minutes, you can set up a program like 1Password that helps you create and use super-secure passwords (think "eAnPGbzoB^E93K&ebrs") and then remembers them for you. It installs right to your browser (Chrome, Safari, etc.) and makes password management literally as easy as clicking a button. Worth the money. Worth the time to read the user guide or watch their clever intro video. Worth *everything*.

PRO TIP

Give someone you love/trust your social media passwords should something happen to you. I have two friends who know exactly what to do with my Twitter profile if I'm no longer able to, er, tweet. And that knowledge gives me some peace of mind.

And there you have it. **Some slick jumping-off points for your digital soul.**

Remember: we're all still learning. This current digital landscape has still only just emerged—a blip in human history. Every day we learn more about how to navigate it, connect with it, and create with it. We're all standing on this mountain, together. Instead of letting that daily avalanche get the best of us, let's all prep a little better for the climb.

MORE KARMA

WHERE TO DONATE/RECYCLE/SHRED JUST ABOUT ANYTHING

Ready for More? If you've been reading in order, you've just learned all about Less, which gave you the tools to declutter the you-know-what out of your physical and digital lives. You're getting closer and closer to being "back to zero"—a better place of clarity and a new start for all great things to come.

Before we explore my favorite ways to keep your creativity and productivity flowing, you've got some additional stuff to get rid of. Aside from all that regular everyday clutter, you may have come across specialty items, or large amounts of paper to shred, or an old computer that—since you've now backed it up to the cloud—can be recycled. Where should you bring or send all this stuff? Who will pick it up? Look no farther than this chapter's handy resource list on page 83.

DO IT NOW

While I want you to know about all the beautiful organizations out there that would love to take your stuff (and the list below is the *short* version!), please

do not *dwell* on which place to choose if it means those items are hanging around even a second longer.

There's no best place or right place.

Just get it out.

(As long as you respect each organization's policies, of course.)

BE SELFLESS

Most organizations offer tax receipts, but some don't. My recommendation: unless it's a really valuable item, let it go regardless of what *you* get in monetary or tax-deduction form. The relief and freedom is your reward. Consider the people who will benefit from your gifts. One person's trash, after all, is another's golden treasure.

And for any given charity or drop-off center, it's not just about who ends up with your old beloved shoes. It's also about the people who work at the charity who have a job to go to every day. Your trip there helps keep all kinds of cycles going.

SAY THANK YOU

When I'm witnessing a client part with something that felt special (or still feels special), you'll usually hear me say "Thank you for your time with us" as the item makes its way into the Donate bin. It's a small but potent acknowledgment that even though it's "just stuff," the emotions embedded in material objects are real. There's a healing and sense of closure that often happens in that moment of gratitude—and a strength-building, too. So don't be afraid to say "thank you" before your belongings set sail.

Want to skip ahead to regularly scheduled reading? To-do lists? Collaboration? Fun? Flip to page 113. And don't forget, all the resources like apps, websites, etc., are in a separate section at the back of the book.

MINI TABLE OF CONTENTS

WHERE TO DONATE

GENERAL STUFF + FURNITURE

Donation Town
Accepts: Home goods, clothes, major appliances, and more.
How: Choose a charity you want to donate to, then work directly with that charity to make arrangements for pickup.
donationtown.org

Goodwill Industries
Accepts: Home goods, clothes, media, sports equipment, furniture, and more.
How: Drop off at stores or call to arrange a pickup.
goodwill.org

Your Local Homeless Shelter
Accepts: Furniture, clothes, home goods, and more.
How: Visit the website to contact homeless shelters in your area to find out what they need.
homelessshelterdirectory.org

Craigslist Free Section
Accepts: Whatever you'd like to offer.
How: Visit the website, post your free item(s), and specify your terms for pickup.
craigslist.org

Freecycle
Accepts: Whatever you'd like to offer.
How: Visit the website, sign up, and post your free item(s).
freecycle.org

WebThriftStore

Accepts: Clothing and home goods.
How: Like eBay for charity. Take a picture of your item, write up a description, and mail it once it's sold. Proceeds go to the charity of your choice.
webthriftstore.com

SELECT CITIES

Pick Up Please / Vietnam Vets

Accepts: Clothes, home goods, and more.
How: Schedule a pickup online. Leave clearly labeled boxes outside your home on pickup day. The driver will come and get all items.
pickupplease.org

Furniture Bank Association of North America

Accepts: Furniture.
How: Visit the website to find a furniture bank near you. Check to see what they accept.
furniturebanks.org

Habitat for Humanity ReStore

Accepts: Furniture, appliances, home goods, building materials, and more.
How: Drop off at stores or call to arrange a pickup.
habitat.org/env/restores.aspx

Out of the Closet

Accepts: Furniture, clothes, home goods, media, electronics, sports equipment, and more.
How: Drop off at stores or call to arrange a pickup.
outofthecloset.org

American Cancer Society

Accepts: Furniture, small appliances, clothes, home goods, and more.

How: Drop off at stores or call to arrange a pickup.

cancer.org/involved/volunteer/discover-shop-locations

Community Warehouse (Portland, Oregon)

Accepts: Furniture, home goods, and more.

How: Drop off items at local sites in Portland and Tualatin.

communitywarehouse.org

National Council of Jewish Women (Los Angeles)

Accepts: Clothes, small appliances, home goods, media, and more.

How: Drop off at stores.

ncjwla.org/council-thrift-shops

Downtown Women's Center (Los Angeles)

Accepts: Clothing, home goods, food, medical supplies, personal care items, and more.

How: Drop off at their location.

dwcweb.org

Housing Works (New York City)

Accepts: Clothes, jewelry, accessories, and more.

How: Drop off at one of their 12 donation centers.

housingworks.org

BABY CLOTHING

Loved Twice

Accepts: Gently used baby clothes.

How: Mail to or drop off at locations in the San Francisco Bay Area.
lovedtwice.org

Baby2Baby (Los Angeles)
Accepts: Gently used baby clothes, breast pumps, bottles, and other baby items.
How: Drop off at one of their locations.
baby2baby.org

BRAS

The Bra Recyclers
Accepts: Clean bras.
How: Fill out the form on their website and they'll email you a shipping label.
brarecycling.com

Free the Girls
Accepts: Gently worn bras of all sizes and styles.
How: Mail or drop off small quantities to one of the locations listed on their site.
freethegirls.org

BUSINESS WEAR + COATS

Career Gear
Accepts: New or gently used men's professional clothing such as business suits, shirts, slacks, and shoes that are currently in style.
How: Mail to or drop off at their NYC location.
careergear.org

Dress for Success

Accepts: New or gently used women's professional clothing such as business suits, shirts, slacks, skirts, and shoes that are currently in style.
How: Drop off at an affiliate.
dressforsuccess.org

One Warm Coat

Accepts: Gently used coats.
How: Search their online directory and drop off at a nearby location.
onewarmcoat.org

WEDDING + FORMAL DRESSES

Adorned in Grace

Accepts: Bridal gowns and wedding accessories.
How: Mail to or drop off at their store in Portland, Oregon.
adornedingrace.org

Brides Across America

Accepts: Bridal gowns less than five years old, unique vintage gowns, and bridal accessories.
How: Complete and submit their form and they will contact you with instructions.
bridesacrossamerica.com

Brides Against Breast Cancer

Accepts: Bridal gowns less than five years old and bridal accessories.
How: Mail to or drop off at their store in Sarasota, Florida.
bridesagainstbreastcancer.org

Princess Project (California)
Accepts: New or gently used prom and formal dresses, jewelry, purses, and wraps.
How: Drop off at one of their locations.
princessproject.org

Bridal Garden (New York City)
Accepts: Clean wedding dresses and bridal accessories that are less than five years old.
How: Make an appointment on their website.
bridalgarden.org

Glass Slipper Project (Chicago)
Accepts: New or like-new prom dresses and accessories.
How: Drop off at one of their locations.
www.glassslipperproject.org

SHOES

Soles4Souls
Accepts: New and used shoes.
How: Start a shoe drive or join one and donate.
soles4souls.org

Nike
Accepts: Sneakers (Nike or otherwise).
How: Drop off at a location near you.
nike.com/us/en_us/c/better-world/reuse-a-shoe

One World Running
Accepts: Running shoes.
How: Mail to or drop off at one of their regional locations.
oneworldrunning.com

ARTS + CRAFTS SUPPLIES

Crazy Crayons
Accepts: Crayons.
How: Mail your unwanted crayons to the address on their site.
crazycrayons.com

Creative Reuse Centers (Select Cities)
Accepts: Arts and crafts supplies.
How: Search for a creative reuse center near you. Here are a few:
Long Beach, California: thelongbeachdepot.org
San Francisco Bay Area: creativereuse.org
Durham, North Carolina: scrapexchange.org
Fort Lauderdale, Florida: trash2treasurefl.org

ARTWORK

Artists for Charity
Accepts: Artwork.
How: Through the mail. Visit the website to see what they will accept.
artistsforcharity.org

Boston Children's Hospital (Boston)
Accepts: Artwork that is framed with plexiglass.

How: Submit a completed Gifts of Art Submission Form with pictures of your artwork. childrenshospital.org/ways-to-help/donate-artwork

BOOKS

Books for Soldiers
Accepts: Used books, CDs, and DVDs.
How: Sign up as a volunteer on the website (required for security) and browse through soldiers' requests.
booksforsoldiers.com

Books for Africa
Accepts: Books, especially reference books, encyclopedias, and textbooks.
How: Mail to or drop off at warehouses in Atlanta, Georgia, or St. Paul, Minnesota.
booksforafrica.org

Pajama Program
Accepts: Nurturing children's books for children in need. (They accept pajamas, too!)
How: Fill out the donation form on their website.
pajamaprogram.org

Book Ends
Accepts: Children's books.
How: Mail to or drop off at centers in Los Angeles. Check online for guidelines.
bookends.org/how-to-donate-books

Your Local Library
Accepts: Books, CDs, and DVDs.
How: Contact them directly to see what they will take.

Discover Books (Select Cities)

Accepts: Books.
How: Drop off at participating centers. Curbside pickup available for more than ten boxes of books. Check online for nearest center.
discoverbooks.com

CARS

Public Radio Stations

Accepts: Cars, boats, motorcycles, trucks, and RVs. Some will take vehicles that aren't working, while others will not.
How: Call your local public radio station to speak with a representative.

Make-A-Wish Foundation

Accepts: Cars, trucks, SUVs, boats, motorcycles, and RVs, whether running or not.
How: Fill out their online form or call to arrange for free towing or pickup within 24 hours.
wheelsforwishes.org

Habitat for Humanity

Accepts: Cars, trucks, boats, RVs, and other vehicles.
How: Call to provide info about your vehicle. Most vehicles are accepted unless the cost of processing and towing exceeds the vehicle's auction value. If it's accepted, they will make pickup arrangements with you.
habitat.org/carsforhomes

Purple Heart Foundation

Accepts: Cars, trucks, boats, SUVs, and other vehicles.
How: Fill out their online form and a representative will contact you to arrange free pickup.
purpleheartcars.org

CELLPHONES

Also see "Recycling + Hazardous Waste" section (page 101).

Hope Phones

Accepts: Cellphones, including broken ones.
How: Visit the website to download a free shipping label.
hopephones.org

Verizon HopeLine

Accepts: Cellphones and accessories.
How: Mail to or drop off at a Verizon Wireless store or a HopeLine phone drive.
verizonwireless.com/aboutus/hopeline

CDS / DVDS / VIDEOGAMES

DVDs4VETS

Accepts: DVDs.
How: Mail to or drop off at one of their VA locations.
dvds4vets.org/donate_dvd.htm

Discs for Dogs

Accepts: CDs and DVDs.
How: Mail to or drop off at their western New York headquarters.
discsfordogs.org

Kid Flicks

Accepts: DVDs of children's movies or television shows.
How: Mail DVDs to Los Angeles location.
kidflicks.org

Get Well Gamers

Accepts: Videogames, videogame systems, and gaming accessories.
How: Mail to or drop off at participating children's hospitals.
getwellgamers.org

ELECTRONICS

Also see "Recycling + Hazardous Waste" section (page 101).

National Cristina Foundation

Accepts: Computers.
How: Visit the website to find a location near you that is accepting donations.
cristina.org

Goodwill

Accepts: Many stores accept both working and nonworking electronics either for resale or recycling.
How: Visit a location near you.
goodwill.org

Music & Memory

Accepts: iPods and iTunes gift cards.
How: Visit the website to download a free shipping label.
musicandmemory.org

EYEGLASSES

New Eyes

Accepts: Eyeglasses, sunglasses, and hearing aids for those in need.
How: Mail to or drop off at their New Jersey location.
new-eyes.org

OneSight

Accepts: Eyeglasses and sunglasses for communities worldwide.
How: Drop off at LensCrafters, Pearle Vision, or Sears Optical.
onesight.org

GIFT CARDS

Plywood

Accepts: Gift cards for those in need.
How: Mail to their Atlanta, Georgia, office.
plywoodpeople.com/projects/gift-card-giver

LINENS

Your Local Animal Shelter or Wildlife Center

Accepts: Towels, bedsheets, comforters, and other linens.
How: Visit the website to find a shelter near you that is accepting donations.
petfinder.com/animal-shelters-and-rescues

MAGAZINES

Your Local Medical Facility

Accepts: Magazines.
How: Call your local hospital, urgent-care center, or doctor's office to see what donations they are accepting.

Your Local Library

Accepts: Magazines and periodicals.

How: Drop off at your Friends of the Library Society. Contact them to see what they will take.

ala.org/tools/libfactsheets/alalibraryfactsheet12

MUSICAL INSTRUMENTS

Hungry for Music

Accepts: Musical instruments, in any condition, other than pianos and organs.

How: Fill out the donation form on the website, and they will contact you.

hungryformusic.org

The Roots of Music (New Orleans)

Accepts: Musical instruments.

How: Call for more information and to see what donations they will accept.

therootsofmusic.org

Mr. Holland's Opus Foundation (Los Angeles)

Accepts: Gently used band and orchestral instruments.

How: Mail in your well-packaged instruments.

mhopus.org

Silverlake Conservatory (Los Angeles)

Accepts: Musical instruments.

How: Contact them for more information and to see what donations they will accept.

silverlakeconservatory.com

OFFICE SUPPLIES

Muscular Dystrophy Association (MDA)

Accepts: Office furniture, office equipment, office supplies, and more.

How: Contact your local MDA branch for more information and to see what they will accept.
mda.org/ways-to-help/product-donation

Your Local School

Accepts: Pens, pencils, paper, binders, Post-it notes, staplers, tape, scissors, and more.

How: Call schools in your area to see what they will accept.

L.A. SHARES (Los Angeles)

Accepts: Office furniture and office supplies.

How: Drop off at their Griffith Park facility or call to arrange a pickup.
lashares.org

SPORTS EQUIPMENT

Pitch In for Baseball

Accepts: Gently used gloves, mitts, bats, helmets, baseballs, softballs, uniforms, and more.

How: Visit the website for info to ship to their Pennsylvania location.
pitchinforbaseball.org/html

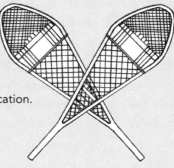

Peace Passers

Accepts: Soccer equipment and gear, including ball pumps, shin guards, and jerseys.

How: Contact them for a current shipment location.
peacepassers.org

Tennis Racquets for Kids
Accepts: Tennis rackets in playable condition.
How: Mail to their location in Great Neck, New York, or drop off there or at other participating New York locations.
tennisracquetsforkids.org

JadeYoga
Accepts: Yoga mats.
How: Drop off at participating regional locations.
jadeyoga.com/store/jades-3-rs-reuse-reduce-recycle-yoga-mat.html

Bikes to the World
Accepts: Bicycles, bicycle parts, accessories, and more.
How: Drop off at participating regional locations.
bikesfortheworld.org

TOILETRIES (+ BEAUTY PRODUCTS)

Hope and Comfort
Accepts: New soap, shampoo, conditioner, deodorant, toothpaste, and more.
How: Mail to or schedule a drop-off time with their Massachusetts location.
hopeandcomfort.org

Clean the World
Accepts: Soap.
How: Mail. Register for a soap drive. Collect soap from your home (and from your consenting friends, if you want). Ship collected soap to centers in Orlando, Florida, and Las Vegas, Nevada.
cleantheworld.org

Beauty Bus
Accepts: New and unused beauty and grooming products.
How: Mail to their California office.
beautybus.org

Your Local Women's Shelter
Accepts: Soap, shampoo, conditioner, deodorant, toothpaste, and more.
How: Call to see what donations they accept. Drop off at a location near you.
womenshelters.org

Your Local Free Clinic
Accepts: Unused or gently used clothes, makeup, skin-care products, and more.
How: Call to see what donations they accept. Drop off at a location near you.

TOYS (+ STUFFED ANIMALS)

Toys for Tots
Accepts: New toys.
How: Drop off at a participating store.
toysfortots.org

My Stuff Bags Foundation
Accepts: Toys, stuffed animals, blankets, clothes, schools supplies, and more.
How: Mail to their California location.
mystuffbags.org/how-to-help/donate-stuff

Gleaning for the World
Accepts: Gently used stuffed animals.
How: Mail to the address on their website.
gftw.org/current-projects/teddybearbrigade

Project Smile

Accepts: Stuffed animals in like-new condition.
How: Mail to or drop off at their Massachusetts location. Check website for donation guidelines.
projectsmile.org/drop.htm

Your Local Day-Care, Religious, or Community Center

Accepts: New and gently used toys.
How: Call to see what donations they will accept.

Stuffed Animals for Emergencies (SAFE)

Accepts: Stuffed animals in like-new condition, children's clothing, baby items, blankets, coloring books, and more.
How: Mail to a SAFE contact listed on the website or drop off with SAFE volunteers in select cities.
stuffedanimalsforemergencies.org

TROPHIES

Awards Mall

Accepts: Trophies, plaques, and awards to donate to nonprofits. (They close seasonally to process donations.)
How: Mail to or drop off at their Wisconsin headquarters.
awardsmall.com/Trophy-Recycling_ep_46.html

Lamb Awards

Accepts: Trophies, plaques, and awards to donate or recycle.
How: Email them for more information.
lambawards.com/recycle.html

Your Local Youth Organizations

Accepts: Trophies, plaques, and awards.

How: Contact local youth organizations (Girl Scouts, sports teams, schools, camps, after-school programs, etc.) to see what they will accept.

RECYCLING + HAZARDOUS WASTE

Earth911

Accepts: Provides comprehensive search and resources to recycle glass, plastic, paper, gardening equipment, construction materials, and more.

How: Use their online directory or call their toll-free hotline (1-800-CLEANUP). earth911.com

Big Chain Stores

Accepts:

BEST BUY: TVs, iPods, MP3 players, car-audio systems, GPS systems, digital cameras, camcorders, mobile phones, CDs, home-monitoring systems, DVDs, e-readers, video-games and consoles, computers, some appliances, pedometers, rechargeable batteries. Varies by state. Check online to see what your Best Buy will accept.

HOME DEPOT: Compact fluorescent lightbulbs (CFLs), rechargeable batteries.

LOWE'S: Aerosols, compact fluorescent lightbulbs (CFLs), fertilizers, latex paint, oil-based paint, pesticides, rechargeable batteries, varnishes, lacquers, thinners, and strippers.

STAPLES: Ink and toner cartridges, certain tech items.

TARGET: Plastic bags, glass, aluminum, MP3 players, cellphones, ink cartridges.

WHOLE FOODS: Batteries.

How: Drop off at your local store.

1800Recycling

Accepts: Plastics, electronics, paper, glass, metal, packaging, hazardous waste, and more.
How: Search for recycling locations using their comprehensive online database.
1800recycling.com

GreenDisk

Accepts: CDs, VHS tapes, PCs, and more.
How: Order a collection box based on weight, then drop it off at your nearest FedEx for pickup. They will safely and securely destroy old data, recover reusable components, and recycle the rest. Visit the website to see what they will accept.
greendisk.com

CD Recycling Center of America

Accepts: CDs, DVDs, ink cartridges, small electronics, and more.
How: Mail by printing out a shipping label from the website.
cdrecyclingcenter.org

PlanetReuse

Accepts: Construction materials and more.
How: Post items on the PlanetReuse Marketplace, where buyers can find materials they need. They'll contact you to coordinate the purchase, pickup, or shipping.
planetreuse.com

Carpet America Recovery Effort

Accepts: Carpets and carpet samples.
How: Find carpet-reclamation partners and locations near you that offer carpet recycling.
carpetrecovery.org/recovery-effort/collector-finder-map

Starkey Hearing Foundation

Accepts: Hearing aids.

How: Mail hearing aids in a crush-proof box or secure package. Be sure to register and insure the package.

starkeyhearingfoundation.org/take_action#/hearing-aid-recycling

Blue Jeans Go Green

Accepts: Jeans and other denim clothes or materials.

How: Mail to or drop off at participating retail stores.

bluejeansgogreen.org

Preserve

Accepts: Brita filters, Burt's Bees lip balm, toothbrushes, and more.

How: Mail by printing out a shipping label, or drop off at eastern U.S. locations. Visit the website to find current partners and what items they will recycle.

preserveproducts.com/recycle/gimme5/gimme5-mail

Local Hazardous Waste Programs

Accepts: Chemicals, cleaners, lightbulbs, oil-based paints, gasoline, propane, and more.

How: Find a waste-disposal site near you.

nrdc.org/enterprise/greeningadvisor/wm-disposal.asp

Local Drive

Many cities now have regular electronics-recycling drives. See if there's one in your area.

Paint Care

Accepts: House paints, primers, stains, sealers, and clear coatings.

How: Drop off at one of their regional locations.

paintcare.org/drop-off-locations

S.A.F.E. Centers (Los Angeles)
Accepts: Residential hazardous and electronics waste.
How: Drop off at a location near you. Check website for hours of operation.
lacitysan.org/solid_resources/special/hhw/safe_centers

SHREDDING

FedEx, Office Depot, Staples Copy & Print
Accepts: Paper for secure shredding.
How: Bring your shredding jobs to any location nationwide.
fedex.com/us/office/shredding-services.html
officedepot.com/a/promo/pages/0307_shredder/
staples.com/sbd/content/copyandprint/idea/officeonthego.html#

Shred-it
Accepts: Paper, hard drives, and media.
How: Find a location near you and request a shredding quote.
shredit.com

ProShred (Select Cities)
Accepts: Paper and hard drives.
How: Fill out the form online for a price quote.
proshred.com/locations

Goodwill Shredding
Accepts: Large jobs of paper and CDs.
How: Call your local Goodwill to see if they offer shredding services. Here's the website for the Southern California location:
goodwillsocal.org/business-services/document-imaging-secure-shredding

SELLING

As I said in chapter 2, *if you're really going to do it*, then by all means—cash is better than clutter. Just give yourself a firm time limit, or else it's Donation City.

eBay
Accepts: Practically everything.
How: Set up an account, then list items with photos and a starting price. Buyers increase their auction bids throughout the week. When an item sells, send it promptly to the buyer.
ebay.com

Craigslist
Accepts: Practically everything.
How: Post items directly on the website. Work out sale details directly with the buyer.
craigslist.org

Move Loot
Accepts: Most types of furniture and select home décor.
How: Submit your items on their site. They'll pick up your item and create your listing. When the consigned item sells, you'll receive a 50% commission (or 70% in Loot Bucks).
moveloot.com

Cash4Books
Accepts: Books.
How: Get a price quote with the ISBN. Ship books with a free label. Payment is issued within two weeks either via PayPal or with a check.
cash4books.net/?ref=351335

Amazon Trade-In
Accepts: Previous purchases, traded in for Amazon gift cards.
How: Follow the instructions on their website.
amazon.com/tradein

Powells (Portland, Oregon)
Accepts: Books.
How: Enter your book's ISBN in the text box and click "sell these books." If they want it, ship to their Portland warehouse. After appraisal, they'll issue payment in online credit or in cash.
powells.com/sellonline

thredUP
Accepts: Clothing, shoes, and accessories, particularly high-end or luxury items.
How: Order a thredUP Clean Out Kit and fill it with like-new clothing. Drop it off at a nearby FedEx Office location for free. They will review your clothes and pay up to 80% of the resale value. Cash out with PayPal or earn thredUP shopping credit. Anything they don't accept will be donated.
thredup.com

LikeTwice
Accepts: High-end clothing and accessories.
How: Request a free Selling Kit and fill it up, then ship it to LikeTwice. They'll make an offer and you'll be paid instantly.
liketwice.com/sell

Tradesy
Accepts: High-quality designer clothes.
How: Order a pre-labeled bag, then fill it and ship it back from your home. They deduct

a 9% commission from your sale, then issue Tradesy Cash for the website or transfer it to your bank account for a 2.9% fee.
tradesy.com

Poshmark

Accepts: Luxury clothing, shoes, and accessories.
How: Create a listing within the app, click the Sell button, take photos of your luxury item, and fill out the info about it. They take a flat commission of $2.95 for all sales under $15 and 20% for sales of $15 or more.
poshmark.com

Threadflip

Accepts: Designer clothing, shoes, and accessories.
How: Send items with their free shipping kit or prepaid shipping label from home. Any items that aren't approved are returned to you by mail or donated to Goodwill. They list all items for you and pay for any items that sell. Cash out with PayPal.
threadflip.com

Bib and Tuck

Accepts: Mid-range to high-end clothing, shoes, and accessories.
How: List your items, and after you make a sale, they take a 15% commission. They'll release funds once you mail your item to the buyer using one of their prepaid labels.
bibandtuck.com

The RealReal

Accepts: High-end luxury clothing, shoes, and accessories.
How: Consign your items with free white-glove pickup in 16 U.S. cities or free shipping via FedEx. Consignors receive 60% of the sale price to start. They inspect and authenticate all items and take care of the selling.
therealreal.com

Crossroads (Select Cities)

Accepts: Mid-range to luxury clothing, shoes, and accessories.
How: Go to a Crossroads store with your items. They choose which ones they want to sell based on the condition of the item and the season. They also offer consignment services for select designer brands.
crossroadstrading.com

Buffalo Exchange (Select Cities)

Accepts: Mid-range to luxury clothing, shoes, and accessories.
How: Go to a Buffalo Exchange store with your items. They choose which ones they want to sell based on the condition of the item and the season.
buffaloexchange.com

Wasteland (California)

Accepts: Mid-range to luxury clothing, shoes, and accessories.
How: Go to a Wasteland store with your items. They choose which ones they want to sell based on the condition of the item and the season. They also offer consignment services for high-end items.
shopwasteland.com

My Little Clothesline

Accepts: Designer children's and baby clothes.
How: Email them for a Vendor Proposal.
mylittleclothesline.com

Nearly Newlywed

Accepts: Bridal gowns.
How: Fill out the form and complete the checkout process (it's $25 to list). They'll promote the sale of the dress, and when the dress sells, you ship it to them and they send you a check for 75% of the net sale price.
nearlynewlywed.com

Still White

Accepts: Bridal gowns.

How: Choose from their Standard or Premium listing ($19.95 or $29.95) and then describe your dress. It'll stay listed until it's sold. Once it is, you keep 100% of the money that it sold for.

stillwhite.com/sell

Decluttr

Accepts: CDs, DVDs, and videogames in good condition.

How: Enter the bar codes for a price estimate. Ship items using UPS or USPS, then get paid by check.

decluttr.com

Local Record Shops

Accepts: Vinyl, CDs, and DVDs.

How: Call to check and see what they will accept.

eCycle Best

Accepts: Electronics.

How: Get a quote on your item, then complete a short form to get a prepaid shipping label. Mail it in, then receive a check or PayPal payment.

ecyclebest.com

Exchange My Phone

Accepts: Cellphones.

How: Describe the condition of your device, then get a quote. If you accept, choose whether you want to get paid or have your money support the charity of your choice. Ship in your phone, and the payment is made via PayPal, with a check, or as a charitable donation. They also accept older or broken phones to be recycled responsibly.

exchangemyphone.com

NextWorth

Accepts: Cellphones, tablets, and other electronic devices.
How: Get a quote on your device (if it's in better condition than described, they pay more), then ship it for free. After it arrives, they make the payment via PayPal or with a check, NextWorth Discover Prepaid Card, or Target gift card.
nextworth.com

uSell

Accepts: iPhones, cellphones, tablets, and other electronic devices.
How: Get a quote. If you take a cash offer, they'll send you a prepaid shipping kit. Get paid via PayPal or with a check.
usell.com

CardCash

Accepts: Gift cards.
How: Tell them which gift cards you want to sell, and get their best offer. Mail in your cards or enter in the gift-card numbers online, then choose check, PayPal, direct deposit, or Amazon gift card for payment.
cardcash.com

Raise

Accepts: Gift cards.
How: Enter in gift-card info and check the balance, then choose a delivery method. Create an account and set up your profile to get paid by check or ACH. Adjust the selling price at any point. Over 90% of cards can be delivered online for free, and the rest get prepaid shipping labels to mail. A 15% commission is deducted from the selling price after the card has sold.
raise.com/sell-gift-cards

Doesn't all that letting-go feel great?
Get used to it. (It feels great every single time.)

MORE PRODUCTIVITY

TO-DO LISTS THAT WORK

Great. All your stuff is finally gone. Or a lot of it. Your small, deliberate, imperfect steps are really starting to make a dent.

One m-a-j-o-r way to help you nurture those newly cleared areas—and help them spur you to creative possibility—is to amp up your productivity. **And the cornerstone of productivity is a well-functioning to-do list** (aka a task list). This is not just about all the little reminders to "buy soy milk" and "pay parking ticket"—though it is absolutely that, too. It's about writing down all the steps to the creative and heart-filled projects you're burning to accomplish. "Stop at nursery for romaine plants to start the garden"; "Ask Karen where she takes ukulele lessons"; "Take ten minutes to look through basement for old skateboard." If you can regularly see all your tasks in one trusted place, it becomes loads easier to plan out your days, your weeks, your wishes, your dreams . . . your life.

A dynamite to-do list is one that you're in constant communication with. It's like an extra limb—the same way your cellphone is, for better or worse. On days that you're checking your email and your calendar (nearly every day, I'd imagine), you should also be checking—and interacting with—your master to-do list. Why? Because you're busy. And the alternatives are time-wasters and energy-suckers. (Rely on different lists in different places, full of duplicates and outdated information? Nah. Remember everything with your *brain*? No, thank you.) Instead, opt for a reliable to-do list that has your back.

First, we'll define the difference between things to *do* and things to *refer to*. Then we'll jump into the simplest ways to set up your master list. Later, I'll introduce you to a concept that can help how you *think* about your to-do list. Because, as with all mountains to climb, this is as much about logistics as it is about a shift in mindset. (And not to worry: this mountain is a gentle hike, with a killer view from the top.)

ACTION ITEMS VS. REFERENCE ITEMS

An action item is something that you must take action on and belongs on your to-do list.

A reference item is something you'd refer to later, like a list of Portland restaurants to visit when you're next in town. For reference items, I use Evernote, a digital notebook app (and so much more) that's super-easy to use.

TIME OUT FOR EVERNOTE!

Evernote is an exceptional way to cut down on paper and brain clutter—tracking all your notes, ideas, and creative sparks. Not everything you need to remember is an actual task with a timeline, so it's helpful to have a digital file cabinet, or reference area, for . . . everything else. Whenever I get ideas for new song lyrics, they go directly into my Lyrics Ideas note within Evernote. Then when it comes time to write new tunes, I can pull up that note on any device and dig in. You might also create Evernote notebooks for things like:

- Storing medical info about family members (What's that medication Grandma's on, again?)
- A list of holiday-card recipients
- Drafts of newsletters you'd like to write
- Scene breakdowns for that TV show idea you've always had
- The instructions to connect your electronics equipment that you always forget
- A record of the types and names of paint you used to redecorate your house (Blue Haze, anyone?)
- Possible band names
- Recipes
- Anything you desire

SETTING UP YOUR TO-DO LIST

I heartily recommend going digital, if you're willing. If you're a smartphone user and can find your way around basic apps like Instagram and iCal, then you can surely find your way around a simple to-do app.

Just imagine: You're out at a party and you remember you need to call your writing partner tomorrow about an important aspect of a project. Instead of hoping you'll remember, you simply pull out your smartphone and input the task with a due date of tomorrow, and it will automatically show up on all of your devices. Then you get to go back to partying (with a clutter-free brain), knowing you're covered.

PRO TIP

While they're great to jot things down quickly, "notes" apps aren't the best choice for a trusted task list. They lack basic (and vital) features like reminding you to do something on a certain day or keeping a record of your completed projects.
Use a simple to-do app instead.

Step 1: Choose one to-do app to try.
There are several great apps on the market. I'll mention only a few because I want you to start ASAP and not get bogged down with too many choices.

FOR IPHONE USERS

Reminders. It's already on your phone! This is Apple's native task-list app, and I've seen it change clients' lives. Double-click on your Home button and say, "Remind me to buy flowers tomorrow at three." And Reminders *will*. You can sync Reminders to your iCloud account (or whatever online enclave Apple switches to by the time you read this) and check your tasks from anywhere.

TO-DO LISTS FOR EVERYONE (INCLUDING IPHONE USERS)

Pick one:

1. Todoist
2. Wunderlist
3. Teux Deux

I would be remiss if I didn't also mention OmniFocus, a first-rate to-do app for Mac/iOS, and the crown jewel of productivity in my own household. It's got quite a few bells and whistles, as far as organizing your task views and overall workflow. If you want to go there—and you'll actually use the thing—by all means, download away. (Watch a few of their how-to videos and your mind *will* be blown. Love you, OmniGroup!) But if this is your first rodeo and you want to start with the most basic functionality, stick with my recommendations above. This is about the fewest steps. This is about *better than before*.

Don't procrastinate for weeks deciding which app to get. **Just pick one.** Literal worst-case scenario: you give it an honest try; you don't like it; you try another. Play around with the features and have fun. Reframe your thinking. This isn't homework for school. This is life. Adult life. Where cool inventions can make it more fun to do all the stuff you've gotta do anyway! And remember: the time you put in now will be made up a *thousandfold* when your efficiency starts to increase.

Step 2: Enter all your tasks and projects into your new app.

Brain dump. It's *on*.

What's the best way to write down a task? **In a word:** *specifically*. As productivity guru David Allen points out in *Getting Things Done*, it's important to use action language when writing down tasks. Not only does the verb propel you into action quicker, but it also breaks down the task into something as tangible as possible. It's hard to wake up one morning and immediately "Get a new car." You have to "Research what my old car will sell for," "Call cousin to see if he wants to buy it," "Ask Marc which dealer he got his Prius from," "Look at available colors," etc. These are all actionable, bite-size tasks: much more digestible, and you can do them a little at a time, which means that you actually will. Those few extra seconds to make tasks specific will rock your future world when it comes time to actually do them.

I write down everything. *Everything.* Weekly trash takeout? Repeating item on my task list. Call curly-haired friend to ask who cuts her hair? Jotted. Buy new ice trays? Check. This way, I almost never have to remember anything. My to-do list remembers *for* me.

Worse Before Better. At first, it may seem overwhelming to look at the list of alllll the stuff you have to do. There may be an uncomfy transition period. Push through it. And once you see everything at the same time, you'll be able to better choose which tasks aren't so imperative after all.

YOUR WANTS ARE TO-DOS, TOO

Write down your wants on your to-do list. Write down your creative tasks, fellow change-makers!

How will you ever write your masterpiece if the steps to get you there aren't clearly laid out?? **Abstract thought is unfortunately not a close friend to productivity.** You might have a dream of joining a woodworking class. ("Oh someday, someday . . .") But the fastest way to get into that class is to write down the logistics to registering. Do it now.

And not to sound like a broken record, but I can't emphasize enough how important specificity is. Jotting down "Write Masterpiece" may help get you a little closer to doing it. But inputting "Spend 60 minutes creating short outline for novel idea" will get you waaaaay closer.

Step 3: Set daily alerts that remind you to interact with your new to-do list.

This will help you get used to your new MO. Once you build the habit and all your to-dos are going into the one app, you won't need the alerts anymore. **It'll be your nucleus.**

Once you find the ones that you like, apps really do work if you work 'em. Say yes to a new thing in your life. And then let it reward you.

DIGITAL VS. PAPER

"But I'm a paper person," you say. Cool. So am I. We need to have tangible things in our lives, and it took me longer than you might think to go digital. But technology has come soooo far. The beauty, delicacy, and sheer magic of a great productivity app can completely change the way you operate.

I've had many a client claim they were paper diehards and then be blown away by what a simple app can do. **They took a risk and felt freed by the switch to digital.**

For true Luddites—you do exist and there ain't nothin' wrong with that—I suggest using ONE master notebook as your all-important to-do list. A legal pad on a clipboard works too. (The clipboard differentiates it from other pads, and you can hang it on the wall if desired.) Whatever you use, make it stand out in some way and revere it as much as you do your wallet and keys. No more permanent collections of tiny notebooks and scraps of paper, *capisce*?

LITTLE PIECES OF PAPER WON'T COMPLETELY DIE, EVEN IF YOU EMBRACE DIGITAL

I get it: you're on a phone call, and you need to jot down information; you just got out of the shower with a brilliant idea, and the pen is closer than your computer. Sometimes writing on paper is just easier. I do it all the time. The *trick* is to then process that paper by transferring the info to the place it belongs. I always have Post-its around and where they're easy to grab. But there's a path those Post-its always follow, à la the middlemen you met in chapter 3. There's *one* small area near my computer where they live before being processed (about once a week). That pile rarely gets high because the time it takes to transfer the info is very minimal. Until then, they're never in danger of being lost, and paper and digital can live in sweet harmony.

PRO TIP

No Visual Reminders

The sweater on the hall table that you keep forgetting to return to your sister? Don't rely on *seeing* the sweater to make you remember—at a certain point, we start to overlook the clutter. Write the errand on your task list. It'll be much more likely to get done.

THE TRIANGLE OF PRODUCTIVITY

Now that you know how to create your new to-do list, let's delve a bit further into a new way of *thinking* about it. **Welcome to the Triangle of Productivity.** Sound the horns. If you're able to hang your hat on this concept, your everyday life will churn out more focus and more freedom. Pretty much guaranteed.

The Concept: everything that requires your attention should find its way into one of three holy places—your email inbox, your calendar, or your to-do list.

Please note that I said "everything that *requires* your attention." (So this is separate from the list of restaurants and paint color info we talked about in the resources section.) This symbolic triangle becomes your **trusted, look-no-further place** for every current responsibility in your life. While it can include things you'd *like* to get done, it absolutely must include all the things you *have to* get done.

EMAIL INBOX

CALENDAR

TASK LIST

TRIANGLE OF PRODUCTIVITY

Giving over to the Triangle means that nothing will fall through the cracks.

Now, don't get scared. This doesn't mean you have to actually *do* everything on your to-do list or reply to every single email. We both know you'll probably never get to every item; no one does. The Triangle concept simply means that if there's something to reply to, a place to be, or a task to handle, you'll be able to find it in one of those three places. And in a world where we now have a thousand different things vying for our attention each day, having three places to *count on* is a decluttered and realistic number. You can decide whether or not to delete, reschedule, or ignore—later.

You won't be perfect all the time, but at least you'll have clear goals.

Most people, in my experience, have a decent relationship with their email inbox and calendar. Not necessarily in the sense that they're well-cared-for, but in the sense that you basically know *how* to interact with these two things. Even if you haven't yet checked out the tips in chapter 4 and your inbox is still a cluttered cesspool, it's still *your* cluttered cesspool. You know how to keep it functioning at a basic level. Likewise with a calendar. But most of my clients do *not* have a functional system for keeping track of tasks and projects, or could mightily improve on their current one. **The goal of the Triangle is to treat your inbox, calendar, and to-do list as equal partners.** Mindset change: GO.

TRIANGLE FUNCTIONALITY

EMAIL INBOX –

How you (mostly) communicate.

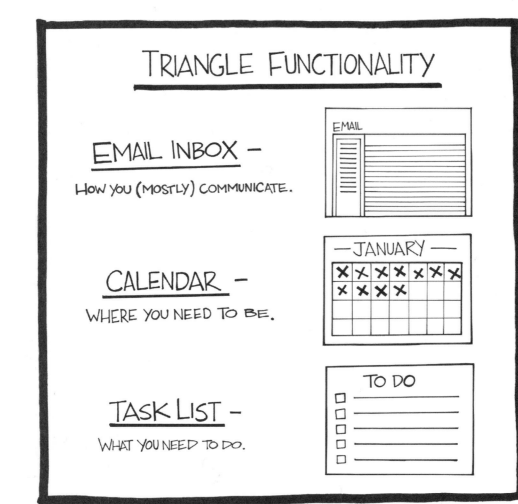

CALENDAR –

Where you need to be.

TASK LIST –

What you need to do.

A NOTE ON CALENDARS

You may have a shared work calendar at the office, a family calendar hanging on the fridge, and a personal calendar on your phone. If your system is working for you, great. But if you're missing appointments or duplicating unnecessarily, schedule a time (once a week, perhaps?) to manually sync all your events into one personal calendar. Take advantage of features like color-coding for different life categories (work, home, creative time, etc.) and the ability to share certain calendars or appointments with certain people.

THREE FRIENDS, WORKING TOGETHER

If you're keeping an email active in your inbox to remind you of something, and it doesn't need a reply, add that task to your to-do list and archive the email. Then, when it comes time, simply search for the email to look at any pertinent info. Use this trick for social media inboxes—like your Facebook messages—as well.

If you're keeping an email active to remind you of a specific event, add the event to your calendar immediately and follow the instructions above. Same holds true for invitations you receive from other sources, like social media.

Or maybe it's a combo platter. You receive a Paperless Post invite to a wedding shower. Within 30 seconds, you can:

1. Follow the link and RSVP
2. Add the event to your calendar (often as easy as clicking a link in the invite)
3. Add "buy wedding shower gift for Hal & Bob" to your to-do list
4. Archive the email so it's out of your inbox

Here's another example: Your friend has emailed you a link to an article you want to read for inspiration on your next creative masterpiece. Instead of the email getting pushed farther and farther down in your inbox, you can:

1. Cut and paste the link into a task on your to-do list, along with "read this article for masterpiece research" and set it to pop up a reminder on Saturday at 10:00 a.m.
2. Create an event to "start masterpiece research" for Saturday from 10:00 to 10:30 a.m. on your calendar
3. Archive the email so it's out of your inbox

Cracks avoided. Clutter gone. Happy explosions.

Your calendar is for scheduled events only, not to record the things you *might* do that day. However, feel free to schedule specific errands from your to-do list. For example, you'll run to the hardware store at 2:30 right before your 3:15 doctor's appointment. Putting specifically timed tasks on the calendar will help you actually do them.

To that end, **scheduling creative tasks for specific times of day, and then treating them like real nonnegotiable appointments, is imperative for productivity.** And for many people, mornings are best to work on anything you are likely to procrastinate on. Knock it out first thing, and that sense of accomplishment and joy will follow you throughout the day. Decluttering the garage this weekend? Building your new website? Put it down for 9:00 a.m., not 3:00 p.m.

PRO TIP

If your texts and voicemails are falling through the cracks, consider adding "text Jack back" or "call Uncle Thom" to your task list.

Less Places to Look = More Productivity

BACKING UP YOUR TO-DO LIST

Most apps sync (and back up) via the cloud, which means that your stuff is saved without you having to think twice. However, you can also usually export the info to a computer file or do a "poor-man's backup" by printing out your list once a week, or by taking a screenshot and emailing it to yourself.

And . . . what if you don't have your info backed up and there's a big crash? Well. Even though you've gone digital, your brain remarkably remembers a ton anyway. It's likely that anything crucial will resurface on its own. So, yes, back up. But more important: breathe. And just don't let the fear of losing stuff keep you from trying out a new system.

DOING YOUR TO-DOS

This chapter is all about setting up your new system and using the Triangle efficiently, strongly anchoring a more productive you. Start getting a handle on that, and you'll naturally cross off a ton of your to-dos. In chapter 8, we'll dig even deeper into exploring ways to grow and sharpen your new healthy habits.

YOU: But what if I can't figure all this stuff out?

ME: Um . . . What if you *can*?

Productivity is not a perfect science.

Two steps forward, one step back is the name of the game. Soon it'll be five steps forward. Then eight. Then eighty.

TRUST THE TRIANGLE.

Then go get some shit done.

MORE HUMAN CONTACT

COLLABORATION + OUTSOURCING

You know who're cool and great? Other human beings.

You know who're cool and great in the specific realms of decluttering your life and accessing creativity and general productivity? *Other human beings.*

By now, you've got a clearer space, a freer brain, and a top-notch to-do list. Let's take it a step further. If you know what you *have* and what you *want*, why not reach out to other people to keep that flow going?

Alone time has its many perks and is often crucial for creative output. But just think about all those exciting projects you'd do if only you had a partner (or partners) in crime. And what about all that stuff you wish you could put on someone *else*'s plate every once in a while?

New and nifty tools keep popping up (thanks, Internet) that can pull in outside help in a variety of ways, supporting our capacity to handle it all— including a robust support network to keep your decluttering on track and cheer you on.

The chapter ahead may feel like a bit of a detour from the New Order you signed up for. But I trust you'll start to see how it's all connected. The two main topics we'll cover are collaboration and outsourcing. There's some overlap between the two, and you can apply whatever speaks to you and let go of the rest.

At the end of the day, this is about involving other people as an *additional tool* for getting shit done (the fun *and* the not-so-fun). **It's about enlisting help, and being braver about doing so. Prepare to get friendly.**

BUDDY UP! (AKA COLLABORATION)

> The downside these days is thinking that "I can do this all on my own." Yes you can do this on your own, but you'll be a much happier human being to do it with other human beings. And I can guarantee you that.
> —MICK FLEETWOOD, in the documentary *Sound City*

High five, Mr. Fleetwood! Collaboration can mean everything from forming a band to starting a business to organizing a chess club. It's a hop on the fast train to getting things done. Often just the reminder that we're *allowed* to involve other people in our projects can open new doors to a world of happy productivity.

So what are you making? What might others help you make? I know you've got something up your sleeve. In many a client's home, I've happened upon an endless array of unfinished projects, in the form of either physical

clutter or mental clutter. "Oh yeah," they tell me, "there's the pile of scripts for that play I've always wanted to mount a reading for." Or, "I desperately want my own blog, but I'm as tech-savvy as someone born in the 1800s, so it's probably not gonna happen."

Sometimes you need long-term collaborators to help you launch creative empires, like rock bands or tech startups; sometimes you need short-term collaborators to fill in the gaps in your know-how, like web designers and film editors; and sometimes you need collaborators who are out there doing the same things as you, to bounce off new ideas and be accountable to, like joining a writing workshop or mastermind group.

Even if you just got *one* step closer to finishing your masterpiece, starting your band, or starting your *brand*, wouldn't that be worth it?

So . . . what's stopping you?

THE FEAR OF REACHING OUT

Talking to other humans? Terrifying. I've lost count of the number of internal pep talks I've had to give myself to write this book (the one you're reading right now!). Audible heartbeats before dialing phone numbers. Anxiously pacing around the house before pressing Send. But slowly and surely—and after many rounds of buddying up—it became, well, real. And done. My name may be on the cover, but there's a rowdy gang hanging out backstage, many of whom I did not know at the beginning of this process. So get your balls on, and let's go meet some folks.

A FEW REASONS YOU MIGHT BE KEEPING OTHER HUMANS AT BAY

- "They won't like my work."
- "They won't like the ideas I come up with."
- "They won't have time."
- "I don't have the cash to pay collaborators or fund a project."
- "If this doesn't work out, I'll feel guilty about it and/or they'll hate my guts."
- "If we create something for profit, it'll be weird to figure out how to split the proceeds fairly."

Or . . .

- "That fancy person is probably totally satisfied in life, and surely too busy for anything else, so it's not worth looking like an idiot and asking if I can create with them or learn from them."

SOLUTION: Play out the worst-case scenario with every "Why not?" (They say "nope"? They want a million dollars? They tell all their friends that you *dared* to reach out about a project? They unfollow you on Twitter?)

Most of my worst-case scenarios go something like this: Fancy Person never calls me back and thinks I'm a ridiculous nobody, and then tells lies about me to everyone I've ever met. Busy Friend resents me for asking for their help, and then never hangs out with me again. You know, the usual absurdities our brains churn out.

Another thing that stands in the way of going out and finding new buddies? The dreaded idea of **networking.** But at its best, the practice simply expands your *network*, your web, and your ability to find who you need when you need them. So if the concept makes you roll your eyes, try changing the lens you're looking through.

> **Redefine "networking."** It's not about "getting connections." It's about *connection*. If you go into a networking opportunity (or a coffee shop, or a party) from a place of exploration and creation, it's a whole new ball game.

And when it comes time to reach out to that very network and ask for help? Why, there are some best practices for doing so . . .

ENTICE THE HUMANS. (Hint: They like food. And gifts. And gratitude.) When you're making "asks" and seeing who might be willing to collaborate or point you in the right direction, it's never the wrong move to sweeten the deal. What you're bringing to the table is surely top-notch, but the person you're looking to connect with might not know that yet. So make it interesting.

A difficult sell: "Hey, can I buy you coffee and pick your brain?"

I am grateful—and shocked—that folks have thought highly enough of me to start asking this on a regular basis. But I'm afraid that the coffee/brain-picking offer is about as enticing as poo on my shoe. Don't get me wrong: I love-love-love giving people decluttering and creative advice (at least to the limits of my own know-how), and I'm constantly on the hunt for my own collaborators. But during a busy life, a few bucks for coffee and one or two hours out of my day is not only not *enticing*, it's often not realistic. (I have to work! And then make time for my loved ones, who are hard to see because *they* work!)

If the ask-ee doesn't yet know how awesome you are, they may wonder—for the sake of their *own* productivity and balanced life—"Well, what's in it for me?" So you gotta give 'em something good, something unique, and something that doesn't feel like a chore. Luckily, that isn't hard to do.

Make it so easy that the other person doesn't have to lift a finger.

A better sell: "Can I hand-deliver you lunch from your favorite restaurant and take 20 minutes of your time to run some ideas past you?"

Huge difference, right? You're going to bring me an entire meal *and* there's a clearly defined cutoff time? Appeal City.

Open-ended can feel overwhelming. Time caps are a strong sell.[4]

---

[4] Have a strong sell, but also be wary of taking it too far. In other words, don't go buying any diamond necklaces. Then it's just weird.

CONSIDER GEOGRAPHY. Go to them. If you're trying to convince some-one to record a sax solo on your new record for half their normal rate, try to choose a studio near their house. Spring for dinner. If you're trying to pitch a project to a blogger who lives in a different city, put yourself in their shoes and think what might be the *easiest* and most efficient way to communicate. Maybe you suggest a 15-minute instant-message session. Maybe a 10-minute phone call that's convenient for their time zone.

DO YOUR HOMEWORK. It would take a total of three minutes to find out exactly what I do for a living, see where I'm from, watch one of my decluttering videos, or listen to a clip of one of my songs. Another two minutes and you can get a taste of my blogging style and see some of the other creative people I collaborate and hang out with. (It's a little creepy that you can do all that, I know, but here we are.) Do as much research as you can before you reach out. It doesn't take long. And if there's *any* info you're looking for that's easily Google-able, do not waste a person's time asking basic questions just so you can "con-nect" with them. It's icky. You can do better.

MAKE THEIR HOMEWORK EASY, TOO. Before a potential collaborator says yes, they will want to find out who the heck *you* are. So, if you're a creative and/or entrepreneurial being out in the world, have a clean and concise webpage that says what you do and lists a way to connect. No bells and whistles necessary. Squarespace, Virb, Weebly, and Wix are all great for do-it-yourself websites. If you can share examples of your work, great. If your impending collaborations are what are going to *create* that work, well, then, you're almost there. Even if you want to do something totally new, show people you have a past: a few lines about the type of work you've done, a photo, contact info—and you're done.

If you've got samples, short pitches, demos, or 30-second videos, that's fantastic. Create easy links for people to click on. No huge files to download. Pretend you're receiving an email from someone. What would be the quickest way for *you* to watch/view/read something?

If you're just out of school, there's no shame in listing what your interests were in high school or college, what you excelled at, and what you're hoping to do moving forward.

Keep emails and voicemails short, sweet, clear, and confident.

DON'T WALLOW IN "NO"S OR LACK OF RESPONSES. We're all trying to juggle as best we can. A "no" or no response at all shouldn't discourage you. Consider that your ask-ee may also be dealing with a cluttered inbox or task list. Many of my clients field multiple requests on a daily basis, and if they responded to every "ask," they'd literally never leave their computers. If you're unable to connect with someone you're eyeballing, it's simply not the right time for you guys to make magic together. Thankfully, we live on a heavily populated planet. Move on.

Getting used to "no"s makes you a more resilient human. Plus, even the folks who say "no" might know a guy who knows a guy!

GET PSYCHED. Palpable excitement about whatever it is you're working on—or whatever it is *they're* working on—is good. Really good. People like to get involved in exciting things with positive energy attached. And they really, *really* like it when what *they* do is exciting to *you*.

WHEN PEOPLE SAY YES, SEND THANK-YOUS (YEAH, IN THE ACTUAL MAIL!). Follow up on how their own projects are going. Remember that their dog just died and check up on them. Small actions like these are worth so much more to people than the effort it takes to do them. After a friend of a friend gave me some free entrepreneurial advice, I sent her a $10 iTunes gift card with a thank-you note, even though there was a voice in my heading saying, "Ten bucks is so cheap. And she'll think it's weird that I'm even being so formal." Instead, I got a gushing voicemail saying how thoughtful I was and how she knew just whose album she was going to buy. Every little bit counts.

These guidelines aren't just for people you deem "more important" than you. (Because that's not a thing. We're all on the same spaceship ride here.) This is a general plan of attack for anyone you're asking for some time or help, regardless of their job title. Humans like to be appreciated. And they want to connect, too.

COACHES + CLASSES + TRAINERS + TEACHERS

Sometimes the most direct line to collaboration is to pony up some cold hard cash. When you work with a trained coach or teacher, you can get to Better faster. Formalizing it a bit also provides ever-important accountability, in the form of scheduled appointments, deadlines, and homework. And even 30 minutes per week can wondrously and dramatically change your life.

When trying to talk myself *out of* taking guitar lessons for the millionth time, I finally exhausted all the usual excuses: lack of funds, no time, "I'll never be as good as [insert virtuoso's name here]," etc. It was time for a very simple, worst-case-scenario query:

"Would you rather die being a kind-of-okay guitar player or no guitar player at all?"

Once I phrased it that way, the answer was obvious: I made the damn call.

Having a teacher keeps me accountable and in communication with another human about my creative appetite. Even when I slack on practicing, that weekly collaboration always gets me back on track.

(Not to mention the whole creative fulfillment / songwriting productivity / waves-of-happy it's launched into my life. No big deal.)

Maybe you've had some urges too. You've said for years that you want to learn Italian or take sewing lessons or know how to properly install a muffler. I can practically *see* those unopened Rosetta Stone CDs on your shelf. And look: there's your unfixed car in the garage, just gathering dust. **By golly,**

the time is now! Don't live near the instructor you want to work with? They probably offer lessons via Skype. Find a way to make it work.

And sure, this book is all about imparting decluttering know-how so you can go at it yourself, but if you want to get to Better even *faster*, consider hiring a professional organizer. That's what we're here for! As with personal trainers and therapists, people employ us because it *works*. If you're waiting for the "right time," give yourself permission to start ASAP. All you gotta do is make the call.

START A CLUB

Or maybe you can start *your own* class! Short on funds? Wanna make it social? Wanna sip whiskey while you jam about the joys of personal betterment? Say, for instance, you want to run with all the stuff you've learned in (*ahem*) this very book, but you're having trouble getting things done on your own and you're not in a position to hire a pro. **Why not start a formal (or informal) group?** I'll bet five or ten of your buds also want to apply some New Order to their lives: weekly check-ins (either in person or with a private Facebook group or Google Hangout) with a game plan and accountability, inspiration to meet your clutter-related deadlines, and an excuse to hang out. (Check out neworderlove.com for more tips on forming a decluttering club.)

REAL LIFE

I'm always floored by how often we forget that we're all going through the same things. When I teach workshops, some of the most frequent feedback is: "I had no idea other people felt the same way"—about creativity, about decluttering, about the fears of posting good news on social media, about everything. And after peeking into people's drawers for the past ten years and speaking to hundreds of creative folks, it's true: **We all have the same stuff—inside and out.**

PHONE A FRIEND

Your friends *like* you, right? And they have desires, too, some of which are pretty similar to yours: to declutter, to create, to live better. If a large gathering of friends feels like too much, what about just one? Maybe your ideal collaborator is already in the Favorites section of your phone.

Don't be someone with regrets. **Make the first move.**

HANDING OFF YOUR TO-DOS (AKA OUTSOURCING)

How else can we get more done? By having other humans do it for us! First, let's broaden our definition of the word *outsourcing*. While it might call to mind underpaid workforces in foreign lands, I use it here to mean, simply: *contracting out work to someone else,* or *delegation.*

OUTSOURCING = TAKING STUFF OFF YOUR PLATE

Doesn't *that* sound like a "less clutter, more productivity" concept if you've ever heard one??

Even if it makes your life just a *little better,* wouldn't that be worth it? Even one or two "extra" hours per week would be marvelous, would they not?

If you've ever gotten a shirt pressed at the dry cleaner, hired a babysitter, or had a pizza delivered, you're already familiar with this concept. And if you are working a job (or seven) and/or have kids and/or struggle to keep up with it all while finding time for happy-making pursuits, further outsourcing = more freedom.

For creative folks, work-from-home parents, and freelancers of all stripes, we don't have the structure of a 9-to-5 corporate office—with receptionists and interns built in—so we have to make up the systems ourselves. It's time to loosen our grip on the status quo. Change the story you've told yourself about what types of things you're allowed to get help with. **Stop doing the stuff that *anyone* can do, so you can start doing the things that *only you* can do.**

We imagine that an assistant is a high-powered luxury meant for *other people.* Please allow me to disabuse you of that idea. The truth is: CEOs and celebrities and anyone with outside help are just regular human beings who get really, really *busy.*

In most cases . . .

It's not about being waited upon; it's about being able to get everything *done.*

Know who else is busy? You. And you, too, deserve a helping hand every once in a while. We're bombarded with stories about "having it all," people who are able to take care of every last thing in their work and personal lives, but, friends, it just ain't reality. And delegating a task doesn't mean we think we're above it, or that we refuse to do it ourselves. You're not skirting responsibility. You're simply decluttering your schedule and releasing some of your everyday burdens so that you can be more attentive to the things that matter most. And navigating a supermarket for two hours on a Saturday afternoon is not one of those things.[5]

So whether it's hiring a part-time (or very *very* part-time) assistant, calling an errand service, or simply having your groceries delivered, consider taking a few things off your plate.

If it makes you feel guilty to have someone do your personal bidding, remember: you are paying them. With money. It's all part of the contract between consenting adults.

---

[5] Unless, of course, you love doing it; then choose something else to outsource, right?

SOME TASKS TO CONSIDER OUTSOURCING

- Grocery shopping/delivery (Farewell, impulse buys!)

- Errand running (mailing packages, dry cleaning)

- Household chores (cleaning, cooking, laundry)

- Pet care

- Travel arrangements/reservations

- Social/party arrangements

- Online research (Where are those woodworking classes you dream of taking? What are the top-rated convalescent homes in Grandma's neighborhood?)

- Gift buying and gift making

- Building your Ikea furniture

- Hanging hooks and shelves (hint, hint)

- Returning emails (it's true!)

- Creative/entrepreneurial tasks (copywriting, marketing, editing)

• **All those things you say you're gonna do, but don't cuz it**

feels too hard

Okay, let's pause a minute for that nice elephant, waving from the corner.

You're still thinking this sounds preposterous. You can hardly afford your monthly subway pass. And I feel you so hard. If you've truly got 0% wiggle room in your monthly budget, this may not be for you—not today, at least. But there's a middle place here. A *vast* middle place. Remember: the manageable and realistic path to a Better life often involves baby steps. Don't wait till your windfall comes in. Do rad shit *now*.

I'm no money expert and you probably shouldn't take financial advice from me. But for what you throw down on a few hand-crafted cocktails, you could have someone fill up your fridge with groceries, while you take a surfing lesson—or a walk.

You must weigh the value of what you're getting. **How much is your time worth? And how much is it worth to know you're doing the things you've always wanted to?** When you have more time and energy, you're a more valuable asset to all of your many life projects—and to the people around you. Period.

Of course, be mindful of your budget. But what's life without a few risks? (Way less fun.) If you have a partner, talk it out with them. Make it clear you're not trying to peace out on your partnership/familial duties. You're attempting to make life more enjoyable, more efficient, and potentially more lucrative down the line—for all of you. (Maybe instead of signing up for surfing lessons, you're building a company!) And if anyone rolls their eyes, remind them that *they're* allowed to do this, too.

WHERE TO LOOK FOR MAGICAL HUMANS

If there's a project you wanna attack, **start talking about it.** It not only makes it *realer* for you, but you never know who's listening. Tell people you wouldn't think to that you're on the hunt for folks to collaborate with. (Or ride bikes with. Or build a neighborhood swimming pool with.) Often, your collaborators are staring you in the face—at work, at school, on Facebook.

REAL LIFE

New Order the business was birthed in 2006 because I wouldn't shut up about, er, wanting to birth it. And soon enough, my big mouth found me colleagues, coaches—and paying clients.

Craigslist has stood the test of time, and remains an exceptional tool to connect people. Or even more old school: put up flyers in coffee shops . . . it still works! See if your neighborhood has a TimeBank, where nice humans barter with one another for everything from Spanish lessons to motorcycle repair. Post requests on social media. Look for a Meetup (a platform that connects local people with common interests and much more). Consider joining a coworking space. They're all the rage, for good reason, and they're not just about having a cool place to do your own work. They're breeding grounds for collaboration, partnerships, creativity, and social enterprise. Google "coworking spaces" and find your tribe. Google till it hurts.

Fear and overwhelm still bubbling up? Find a nugget of confidence—or fake it. And remember that you're not going to be around forever. (No pulled punches here.) Might as well grab some buddies and enjoy the ride.

MORE PLACES TO FIND COLLABORATORS/FOLKS TO OUTSOURCE TO/EVERYTHING IN BETWEEN

- **Craigslist.org: the original online bulletin board**

- **hitRECord.org: an open, collaborative production company; artists of all types collaborate and share in the profits**

- **Upwork.com: business and design help, virtual assistants**

- **Freelancer.com: ditto**

- **Behance.net: find designers of all types**

- **Dribbble.com: a show-and-tell for designers**

- **99designs.com: find graphic designers (mostly)**

- **NAPO.net: find professional organizers and declutter specialists (with a long list of niches)**

- **APPO.org: find personal photo organizers to help you take charge of your thousands of photos, physical and/or digital**

- **TaskRabbit.com: outsource household tasks, home specialists (cleaning, handypersons, repair, lawns), general assistance**

- **Fiverr.com: outsource everything from social media help to having someone wish your kid happy birthday in a Harry Potter accent. (I suggest tipping extra and doing the gig "add-ons" for a more equal exchange.)**

- **VirtualStaffFinder.com: for entrepreneurs who want to find top-notch virtual assistants**

- **FancyHands.com: a monthly subscription gives you a certain amount of requests ("call the cable company for me," "research things to do in my mother-in-law's town") and fulfills them via their huge network of assistants**

- **Postmates.com: on-demand delivery from local stores and restaurants**

- **Instacart.com: grocery delivery with low fees, open 'til midnight**

- **Peapod.com: grocery delivery and pickup**

- **AmazonFresh.com: delivering fresh groceries and Amazon products**

Please note: some of these in-person services are still growing their areas of delivery and may not yet serve your neck of the woods. Why not see what your local businesses are up to first? Maybe your neighborhood pharmacy just started delivering or there's a new CSA (community-supported agriculture) that offers pickups just down the block.

REAL LIFE

I have a trusty helper myself. And I hired her "before I should have," financially speaking. Spending that money before paying off some of my debt just seemed plain dumb. But there was a nagging truth that quite literally kept me awake at night: I was spreading myself way too thin. I decided that if delegating worked, I'd have more time and energy for work, clients, and creativity. *And* that if I really couldn't afford it, I'd know after a few months and could chalk it up to experience.

Needless to say, it's the single best decision I've made for my life, my career, and my general well-being.

Delegating errands ("Please drop off this Amazon return to the UPS Store") and online research ("Please send me info for the three most highly rated dentists within a five-mile radius") has freed up time for—among many other things—more client sessions, digging deeper into creative and business strategies, and *rest*. And collaborating on projects like my monthly newsletter has made me a better writer (by getting editorial feedback before hitting Publish), while keeping me accountable to actually send it out. Our work together has nothing to do with being fancy, and everything to do with productivity.

HOW TO DECIDE WHAT TO PAY

This amount will depend on the services and your freelancer's qualifications. Some people will tell *you* what they charge. If you are hiring a part-time assistant and it's your call, ask around to see what the going rate is in your area. Do some Googling. Put yourself in your hiree's shoes. In some cities, $15 per hour isn't even considered a living wage, but in others that's a generous place to start. Again, there are variables. Follow your heart. Lastly, please check with your tax pro on how to classify them (employee vs. independent contractor), which may depend on how much your new helper is working and what they're doing for you.

PRO TIP

To share project info and delegate tasks, I use an app called Trello. Instead of letting important details get buried in multiple emails, we can both send everything pertinent (with attachments, even!) straight to a private digital workboard. Simple and efficient. Asana, Basecamp, and Slack are great, too.

Project-management apps are useful for collaborations of all kinds. As important as your email inbox is, even one with a fantastic search function can be a time-suck for finding important info. With these apps, you've got the necessary info at your fingertips. It's much easier for me to go to my project page and see exactly what's being worked on.

PRO TIP

Many of the aforementioned websites vet their freelancers, but if you're handing over any personal info or documents, or if you're giving out a key to your house, I do suggest you do whatever type of background checking and/or precautions you feel are necessary. (If there's anything you don't feel comfortable sharing, do not share it.) And then take the exciting plunge.

In most cases, your "transactions" will go smoothly. But like any life change, the process might be uncomfy at first. You and your collaborators/freelancers/outsourcees have to learn how best to communicate, and that may take a few tries. Just like the clutter in your house, it might get a little worse before it gets better. But boy, is the payoff sweet.

Be kind, be clear, be flexible.

And have fuuuuun.

8

MORE PRACTICE

HAPPY HABITS + JOYOUS RETURNS

While I stand strongly by the power of small steps, let's also give it up for thinking *big*. Because all those steps lead to a new way of EXISTING. They add up to *major stuff*. (Major good stuff.) After you cleaned out your closet, you unearthed the old easel and started painting again, perhaps aided by the small step you took to schedule a painting session every Wednesday morning. It is *all connected*, folks. And it's ongoing . . .

Remember: Even in the best-case scenario in which you curb your shopping habits and become happier with less, you will still acquire *some* new things—and you will lose the need for some of the old.

Life changes. Your needs will change. Your rooms will change. Your desires will change.

So this final chapter explores ways to nudge ourselves (or sometimes shove ourselves) into those small-step actions, over and over again, until they become second nature.

......never mind.

If you have already felt a surge of adrenaline and taken immediate action, *hurray*! If not, you'll start to reap the happy rewards as soon as you do. You'll feel it in your bones. It's palpable—and it can be addicting. But it's also not unusual for the initial buzz to fade after a few weeks or months. Do not despair. It's a *process*. And patience will serve you well.

REAL LIFE

Often a client will get such a thrill from the decluttering process we start together that they keep going long after I leave. I'll return for our next session and they'll actually feel *guilty* that they've already dug through the things we were supposed to work on that day. Of course, nothing pleases me more than seeing this initiative, this excitement, this fervor. 'Tis the very goal of New Order. (And never once have I looked at their "work" and thought they've done it "wrong.") But what gave them the drive was not *me*. It was doing the work at all.

FORWARD MOTION!

The word I used to use to refer to "keeping up with decluttering" was *maintenance*. "You do all this work, and then later you'll just need to maintain it," I would say. But at some point I realized that none of that sounds enticing, easy, or fun. It sounds stressful. The path to your sweeter life is not actually about *maintaining*, which is a reflection of what you did yesterday. It's about forward motion and new practices, which are a reflection of how you want to live today—and tomorrow. There are no pasts to re-create. You're simply building upon what came before, to keep your present and future self happy and productive.

Instead of leaving them scattered around your office, you're putting the painting supplies back in their new home because that'll help you today, and next week. You'll purge the pantry again in six months because you're an imperfect human who didn't get around to eating every last thing before it expired. But this time it'll take you only 5 minutes instead of 45.

Just like taking a yoga class or getting a good night's rest, these are healthy practices. And healthy practices lead to feeling better. Plain and simple.

**Adopting the decluttered life isn't a chore.
It's a fun way to be alive.**

Imagine being able to shout from the mountaintops:

"I GET to know where everything is! I GET to have fewer emails in my inbox and not be pestered by hordes of newsletters! I GET to look at only one to-do list and know that I'm not forgetting anything! I GET

to make stuff I like with people I like! I GET to pass off a task every once in a while! I GET to donate stuff I DON'T NEED to places that DO! And I GET to make this a lifestyle, for as long as I so choose— because I'm the boss of everything I do! *Yeehaw!"*

You'll enter a new stage of your life, where things like donating clothes and asking for help and managing a to-do list start to feel natural—even sublime. I know it's possible because I see it happen all the time, in my clients' lives and in my own.

Practice doesn't make perfect.

Practice makes better.

Practice makes *glee.*

REAL LIFE

On the regular, I receive out-of-the-blue texts, emails, and photos from my clients, proudly reporting progress they've made since we worked together. Sometimes, I'll even hear from someone years later, letting me know that they still adhere to the systems that we created, or that they're doing a big purge using principles I shared. This doesn't mean that their homes have remained spotless—but they've remained *better than before.*

YOUR NOW HABITS

In order to adopt new practices, we have to assess our current habits. Habits and practices aren't inherently good or bad. They're just actions our bodies and minds get used to, for better or worse.

Take some time to acknowledge what you're *used to* doing. This is one reason why I tell clients not to clean up before I come over. That way, we can work with their current habits to decide on new or adjusted ones, instead of re-inventing the wheel.

For instance: if you tend to get work done better at the kitchen table than in your office, then work at the kitchen table! This doesn't mean, however, that your piles of work have to live there, too. Consider *why* you gravitate toward certain areas. I've had many clients who hated working at their desks simply because the lighting was poor. Small changes—like buying an affordable lamp— can make major differences.

Acknowledge your NOW habits. Then you can start adopting your NEW habits.

YOUR TOOLS: AT THE READY

Next, assess your permanent pregame setup. And how you can make each small step as easy as possible. We talked about accessible storage of your magic tools in chapter 2, but what's their current level of functionality? Think about your larger supplies and instruments, both figurative and literal. What can you do to make using them even simpler? Are you a writer who is so used to cursing your fussy printer that you've forgotten it's possible to have one that actually *works*?

A mandolin player who has had a string missing for years, even though you keep meaning to get to the music store that's right down the street?

PRO TIP

Upgrade (or fix) your basic tools.

Working tools = working productivity

= easier to PRACTICE YOUR HAPPY/CREATIVE/ PRODUCTIVE LIFE.

Your tools need to be fired up and ready to operate at a moment's notice. If I stored my guitar in its case, I would never take it out every day to practice. Heck, no. It's on a guitar stand. Right in the middle of the living room. With nothing blocking it. Staring me in the *face*.

NEW PRACTICES CATCH ON QUICKER THAN WE THINK

Some practices may take several months to feel natural. But some can catch on in the blink of an eye. As an exercise in putting my money where my mouth is, I decided to start playing music first thing each morning while writing this book, for a minimum of 15 minutes every time. This felt like an easily digestible and realistic amount of time to start with, and as you might guess, I would often go much longer.

Miraculously, by day six, any tendency toward resistance and procrastination was replaced with an unconscious *knowing* that, after my alarm went off and I brewed some chai, it was time to walk over to the piano, because the muscle memory had already set in. And because I was already reaping the joyous rewards.

Other examples of a daily morning practice might be a walk, a meditation, putting the living room back in order. Again, it could take weeks or months for you to start feeling that natural flow. But once it *does* catch on, your brain chatter gets to stop working so hard, and your body is all, "I'll take this from here." Science!

A RULE IS COOL

Remember the concept of parenting yourself from chapter 4? Well, that technique also applies to, um, everything else. It's cool to have some rules every once in a while. **In adulthood, a rule is just a conscious choice.** No more rigid childhood connotations of "following the rules" and "staying in line." Nope. It's just saying out loud *what you would rather have happen than not.* And then living that.

It's about creating templates for how you want life to go. Alternatively, we're left with no road map and huge piles of indecision.

Think about all the little things you never actively chose: where the mail should land, or how many toilet paper rolls is too many. **Sometimes changing a habit is as easy as making the unconscious conscious, and deciding on a new rule.** Don't think of it as being inflexible: you're free to tweak or break the rule later as it suits you.

REAL LIFE

I threw my clothes on the bedroom chair for a very long time, and the pile would bum me out whenever I glanced over. It finally occurred to me that unless I made a rule to NOT do it, then my habit would never change. I actually said out loud: "Hey. Chair. You are not for clothes. You are for me to sit in, comfortably. I want to be able to *see* you and *use* you when I walk into my bedroom (for relaxing in and supporting my buttocks while I play music). So I will no longer throw clothes on you. I will hang them up or throw them in a designated in-between bin in the closet instead."

. . . I've had only one slip-up since. Them's pretty good odds.

CREATE THE STRUCTURE + DRAW THE LINES. (AND THEN FEEL FREE TO COLOR OUTSIDE THEM LATER.)

ENTICE YOURSELF

If it feels challenging to get to the all-important starting bell, don't be afraid to set yourself up for tangible rewards. When there's an offer on the table, what are the types of incentives that get you to raise your hand and say, "Me, me! I want that!"? Maybe it's buying yourself a ticket to a sports game. Or a monthly spa visit. Or a night of watching three Cameron Crowe movies uninterrupted.

Bargaining with yourself to get results? Completely acceptable. "I'll clean out my car the first Saturday of every month. And then I'll buy myself an ol'-fashioned ice cream cone." Yeah you will. And it'll taste so so sweet.

TRY A LITTLE HARDER

Here's the thing: **you know what to do.** You know that if you wrote one page of your novel every morning, or did the dishes every night, you'd feel better. There's only so far our excuses can take us. But it's a daily practice to—in the very moment of resistance—push past "I don't wanna" to that *next second* of picking up the journal and pen. Or the dirty dish and sponge.

Just try a *little* harder. I'm always reminding myself that it takes only seven more seconds to hang up those two pieces of clothing each night, so that two pieces don't later turn into twenty. And it takes a mere three minutes to practice an old song. Sometimes the formula is almost too easy.

This particular phrase has proven effective for many of my clients, and though I always worry the words sound too harsh, I'm assured that they know exactly what I mean. Similar to "What's the worst that could happen?," "Try a little harder" is one of those seemingly simple yet jaw-droppingly effective prompts to propel us into action.

FOR F*&K'S SAKE, BELIEVE!

If you don't believe that any of these glorious changes are possible, then we can all just go home (to our cluttered homes, at that). And **pretending that all our psychological junk isn't a part of every step in this process is ignoring the heart of the matter.** That said, the practice of believing ain't always easy. So don't beat yourself up if those naysaying voices toy with your emotions on a regular basis.

Sometimes we simply don't believe we can, or that we're allowed. And sometimes we worry that if we DO, other people will think we're trying to prove something, to be better than they are. When really we're just trying to *enjoy our lives*—which we keep waiting on permission for. Who are we waitin' on??

And man-oh-man: It can feel like there's a very fine line between loving yourself (and *taking care of yourself* and your space) and being narcissistic. Between rightly celebrating your accomplishments (everything from "Come rejoice in the beauty that is my linen closet!" to "Isn't it cool that my art piece just got put in a fancy show?!") and showing off.

But only you know what's true and what feels good and right. So if any of *that* inner clutter is blocking your next steps and new practices, take some deep breaths and walk through it. Believe that change is possible.[6]

---

[6] Didn't know you were reading a hippie self-help book this whole time? Surprise!

REAL LIFE

"Who am *I* to write a book, spread my ideas, share a song, charge what I charge, live a decluttered life, attempt to take care of my health, be (*gulp*) happy? That's for other *better* people, not me."

. . . **Oh, I'm very familiar with the not-believing stuff. And let's call a spade a spade— the unworthiness stuff. Every person who has ever existed is familiar with it. So it's become a *daily decision* to believe I can do what I want, how I want. (And deserve to.)**

As long as I'm nice to people and myself . . . my only caveats.

WHAT LIES AHEAD

In the next few pages, you'll find a handy recap, with the headlines from each of the previous chapters. Feel free to flip to it anytime you need a cheat sheet or gentle nudge.

What lies ahead *outside* this book? I leave that up to you, good folks. Here's to it being a happy, decluttered, imperfect version of your own New Order.

This life . . .

This ride we're all on . . .

This whole thing is a practice.

Practice for what?

For the next day, I suppose.

For the joy that comes with the attempts.

For being **a little better**.

SEE YA OUT THERE.

(And thanks.)

THE RECAP

BEFORE YOU BEGIN

- If you're stuck getting started, remember your *whys*. How do you want to feel as a result of the decluttering process? Focus on the reward instead of the task at hand.
- You can get more than you think done in 10-, 20-, or 30-minute chunks of time.
- Timers are your friends. Use them for accountability and action.
- Just start. (It's the hardest part.)

1 LESS STUFF

- Set up and label your sorting categories. Start with Donate, Recycle, Trash, Shred, and Other Rooms. One by one, simply toss each item into one of the piles.
- Sort your Keepers on a nearby surface and group like items together (batteries with other batteries, etc.). Use Post-its to label categories.
- Be *brutal* about letting go. If you wouldn't fall into a deep depression if it was gone *and* you don't use it, then it's dead to you.

2 LESS "WHERE THE F*&K IS IT?!"

- There's no "right place" to store anything, as long as you (and your cohabitants) know where to find it.
- Make frequently used items accessible and easy to grab.
- Containers don't have to be pretty (unless you want them to be). Repurpose things you already have. Shoe boxes are a godsend.
- Label containers and boxes as specifically as possible ("Guitar Accessories" as opposed to "Music").
- Donate immediately and often. Choose to sell only if you're *really gonna do it*. (Or *really gonna* get someone else to do it for you.)

3 LESS PAPER

- Desks are for creating and working, not for piles.
- Sort paper into: File, To Do, Recycle, and Shred.
- Save only the reference papers you *really* need to keep. And don't place anything on top of your files.
- "Middlemen" are temporary homes for your action-oriented paper. Use wall files and/or magazine files for this purpose—and label them!
- Open your mail daily and cancel all your catalogs and subscriptions to unread magazines.
- Thumbs-up for paperless billing.

4 LESS DIGITAL

- Reassess your relationship with digital life by deciding what you *want* from it.
- Start fresh with a clean email inbox by archiving everything you no longer need.
- Unsubscribe like it's your job.
- Turn off social media notifications and make your use of social media a conscious choice.
- Use apps that help police your digital usage.
- Back up your devices—ASAP.

5 MORE KARMA

- Use this chapter's resource list to your heart's content to give away as much stuff as possible, as *soon* as possible.
- It doesn't matter how much you paid for it. Share it with someone else who needs (or wants) it more.
- "Thank you for your time with us" is a great mantra when letting go of your discards. Sure, it's just "stuff." But maybe it meant something to you, and you can get closure by acknowledging that and saying farewell.

6 MORE PRODUCTIVITY

- Say hello to your new, trusted to-do list (in digital form, if you're game).
- Write down all tasks and desired projects on that one to-do list.

- Think about your email inbox, calendar, and to-do list as a Triangle of Productivity, and say goodbye to things falling through the cracks.
- Visual reminders are not your friend. Write everything down.
- Use Evernote for reference items, like creative ideas and favorite restaurants.

7 MORE HUMAN CONTACT

- Other people are GREAT! Use them to help you be more productive and creative.
- Make it easy for people to want to buddy up with you, by doing your homework and taking their busy schedule into consideration.
- Hire coaches and teachers. Take classes. Start or join clubs.
- Declutter your schedule by outsourcing to other folks, focusing on things that only you can do.

8 MORE PRACTICE

- Ongoing practices are not about maintaining the past. They're about forward motion and making life easier today—and tomorrow.
- Upgrade or fix your basic tools, so work becomes easier and breezier.
- Rules are cool. Create the template for how you *want* life to go by making conscious decisions about new habits and practices.
- If it's hard to get started, entice yourself with tangible rewards.
- Believe all this stuff is possible, and the decluttered life is yours.

APPS, WEBSITES + ADDITIONAL RESOURCES

The digital world moves so fast, and some of these apps and resources may no longer exist by the time you read this. If that's the case, spend a few minutes Googling and/or stay current with me at neworderlove.com.

TIMERS (BEFORE YOU BEGIN)

My timer of choice is tomato-timer.com, based on Francesco Cirillo's celebrated Pomodoro Technique, which promotes working for 25 minutes at a time, only on the task at hand, and with *zero* interruptions. (This whole book was written in 25-minute increments.) There's a system for breaks, too—remember how important those are!—and I encourage you to dig deeper at pomodorotechnique.com. Or, for decluttering or any other tasks, feel free to use the basic timers on your smartphones.

SORTING AND FILING SUPPLIES (1-3)

(These are examples only.)

- **Folding mesh cubes:** containerstore.com
- **Super Sticky Post-its** (yellow, 3x3) + **black Sharpies:** staples.com; amazon.com; your local office-supply shop
- **File crate:** Staples File Storage Crate, staples.com (approx $8)
- **File box:** Open-Top File Box, containerstore.com (approx $6)
- **Hanging files:** Staples Colored Hanging File Folders, Letter, staples.com (all one color, box of 25, approx $16)
- **Letter opener:** staples.com (approx $2)
- **Wall files (or Wall pockets):** containerstore.com; amazon.com; staples.com
- **Magazine files:** containerstore.com; ikea.com

DOWNSIZE AND ARCHIVE YOUR KIDS' ARTWORK (1)

- Artkiveapp.com

MY FAVE PRODUCTS—AFTER YOU'VE DECLUTTERED! (2)

- **Undershelves/undershelf baskets:** containerstore.com; amazon.com
- **Wall shelves:** almost everywhere! I like the Ekby shelves from ikea.com
- **Hooks:** your local hardware store; amazon.com; anthropologie.com; restorationhardware.com
- **Small trays:** your local thrift store; ikea.com; worldmarket.com
- **Archive safe boxes:** exposuresonline.com

TAKING INVENTORY OF ALL YOUR STUFF (2)

- Binaryformations.com/products/home-inventory

GETTING OFF (PAPER) MAILING LISTS (3)

- Catalogchoice.org: cancel your catalogs from one handy site
- Paperkarma.com: app to stop unwanted mail
- DMAchoice.org: snail mail and email opt-out
- Optoutprescreen.com: opt out of credit-card and insurance offers
- coxtarget.com/mailsuppression/s/DisplayMailSuppressionForm: remove yourself from Valpak mailings

DIGITALLY ARCHIVING YOUR MONTHLY STATEMENTS (3)

- Filethis.com

FINANCES AND BUDGETING (2 AND 3)

- Mint.com
- Ourfreakingbudget.com

SCANNING APPS (3)

- Genius Scan (thegrizzlylabs.com)
- Scanbot (scanbot.io)
- Scannable (evernote.com/products/scannable)

PAPERLESS RESOURCES (3)

- Documentsnap.com
- Macsparky.com

UNSUBSCRIBING FROM EMAIL LISTS (4)

- Unroll.me
- Mailstrom.co

DAILY EMAIL FLOW AND SCHEDULING (4)

- Mailboxapp.com: easily swipe messages away and decide when they return
- Boomeranggmail.com: control when you send and receive messages
- Inboxpause.com: put your email on "pause"
- Rightinbox.com: schedule emails to be sent later

POLICING YOUR DIGITAL USAGE (4)

- Anti-Social.cc
- Macfreedom.com
- Selfcontrolapp.com

SOCIAL MEDIA SCHEDULING (4)

- Buffer.com
- Hootsuite.com

COMPUTER BACKUPS (4)

- Backblaze.com
- Code42.com/Crashplan

FILE SYNCING ACROSS DEVICES AND FILE SHARING (4)

- Dropbox.com

PASSWORD MANAGEMENT (4)

- Agilebits.com/OnePassword
- Lastpass.com

DIGITAL FILE CABINET / NOTEBOOKS (6)

- Evernote.com

DIGITAL TO-DO LISTS / TASK MANAGEMENT (6)

- Reminders (iPhone users: it's already on your phone.)
- Teuxdeux.com
- en.todoist.com
- Wunderlist.com
- Omnigroup.com/omnifocus (more functionality, Mac/iOS platforms)

DIY WEBSITE BUILDERS (7)

- Squarespace.com
- Virb.com
- Weebly.com
- Wix.com

COLLABORATING / PROJECT MANAGEMENT (7)

- Trello.com
- Asana.com
- Basecamp.com
- Slack.com

Disclaimer: Every resource listed in *New Order* I've either used or heard nice things about. None of these companies have paid me, nor can I take responsibility for any of their malfunctions or disappearances. Happy decluttering.

DONATE	**DONATE**
RECYCLE	**TRASH**
SHRED	**OTHER ROOMS**

YES, THERE ARE TWO DONATE LABELS ON PURPOSE.
(GET RID OF STUFF.)

A VERY BIG THANK-YOU

To my (dear, brave, trusting, hilarious, creatively spectacular) Clients; to Nina Shield, soul sister editor, and the exquisite Ballantine team; to Katherine Latshaw and Rachel Miller—the sun and moon for you; to Jeremy Gates—from Claflin to this . . . what an honor. To my beautiful Mom, David, Louise, Bill, Maurice, Family, and Friendships; to Jesse Hara, Zibby Allen, Nadia Osman, Karen Kondazian, Joshua Ostrander, Rachel Wolf, Pamela Ribon, Rebecca Feldman, Jay Reiss, Jon Granat, Jeni Rinner, and Daniel Zaitchik.

To the gang at Apartment Therapy; to all who have lent your names and praise to this project; to my NAPO colleagues (especially Beth Penn and Deron Bos for your gracious help); to all creative collaborators and teachers and inspirers; to New Order, the exceptional band; to You, the reader; and to . . . everyone else.

With buckets of love.

xFW

INDEX

FAY WOLF founded New Order, her decluttering business, in 2006. Since then, she's guided hundreds of creative folks (and everyone else) toward less inner and outer clutter, more creativity and productivity, and maybe even a happier adulthood. She has a One-Minute Tip video series with Apartment Therapy and has been featured as an expert on OWN Network's *Home Made Simple*. As an artist, Wolf digs through her own clutter to release songs and creative projects out into the world. Her sad tunes, available on iTunes and Spotify, have been heard on a long list of TV shows, including *Grey's Anatomy* and *Pretty Little Liars*. She's also acted on stages across the United States, and in shows like *2 Broke Girls* and *Bones*. Wolf is a Golden Circle member of the National Association of Professional Organizers and lives on the West Coast.

neworderlove.com
Instagram.com/faywolf
@faywolf